JULIO GONZALEZ

BY MARGIT ROWELL

The exhibition is supported by grants from the National Endowment
for the Arts, Spain–U.S. Joint Committee for Educational and
Cultural Affairs and the Ministry of Foreign Affairs of Spain.
Additional funding has been received from the Arthur Ross Foundation.

THE SOLOMON R. GUGGENHEIM MUSEUM, NEW YORK

JULIO GONZALEZ

A RETROSPECTIVE

Published by

The Solomon R. Guggenheim Foundation, New York, 1983

ISBN: 0-89207-039-0

Library of Congress Catalog Card Number: 82-062612

© The Solomon R. Guggenheim Foundation, New York, 1983

THE SOLOMON R. GUGGENHEIM FOUNDATION

THE SOLOMON R. GUGGENHEIM MUSEUM

LENDERS TO THE EXHIBITION

Dr. W. A. Bechtler, Zollikon

Mrs. Andrew Fuller, New York

Paul Haim, Paris

Hans Hartung, Antibes

M. K. Hoss

The Arthur and Madeleine Lejwa Collection,
New York

Mr. and Mrs. Brian Leyden, New York

Carmen Martinez and Viviane Grimminger, Paris

Adele and Irving Moscovitz, New York

Estate of Joaquín Torres-García

Louise Varèse, New York

Branco Weiss, Zürich

Winston-Malbin Collection, New York

Association Fondation Christian et Yvonne Zervos,
Vézelay

The Art Institute of Chicago

The Baltimore Museum of Art

Fogg Art Museum, Harvard University,
Cambridge, Massachusetts

Fondation Maeght, Saint-Paul-de-Vence, France

Hirshhorn Museum and Sculpture Garden,
Smithsonian Institution, Washington, D.C.

Kunsthalle Bielefeld

Kunsthaus Zürich

Wilhelm-Lembruck Museum der Stadt Duisberg

Moderna Museet, Stockholm

Musée des Beaux-Arts de Nantes

Musée National d'Art Moderne, Centre Georges
Pompidou, Paris

Museo de Arte Moderno, Barcelona

Museo Español de Arte Contemporáneo, Madrid

The Museum of Modern Art, New York

The Museum of Fine Arts, Houston

Philadelphia Museum of Art

Rijksmuseum Kröller-Müller, Otterlo

Staatsgalerie Stuttgart

Stedelijk Museum, Amsterdam

The Tate Gallery, London

Galerie Beyeler, Basel

Galerie de France, Paris

David Grob, London

The Pace Gallery, New York

TABLE OF CONTENTS

Paris, ca. 1909-10

ACKNOWLEDGEMENTS

It is difficult to bring together a comprehensive and coherent selection of a major artist's oeuvre, particularly when that oeuvre is relatively restrained and, with the exception of a few museum collections in which it exists in quantity, is disseminated across two continents. The difficulty and importance of the task is increased when an artist is regarded as a seminal figure and his work is prized as exemplary in the founding of a major modern style. Such is the case of Julio González.

González's impact on twentieth-century sculpture need not be argued today. Over the past three decades assembled metal sculpture has emerged as the dominant sculptural idiom in the West, particularly in England and America. And González, both in his collaboration with Picasso and in his independent work throughout the 1930s, was the artist who invented this new language of form. Yet his oeuvre has not been given a major showing in the United States since The Museum of Modern Art retrospective in 1956, twenty-seven years ago. The original sculptures have not been presented in breadth and depth in Europe since the fifties. None of these exhibitions were as ambitious as the present undertaking.

We must therefore express our sincerest thanks to all those who have participated in this endeavor. Our gratitude is first of all extended to Margit Rowell, Curator of Special Exhibitions at the Guggenheim, who organized the exhibition and wrote the present catalogue. Her sensitivity to González's oeuvre, her indefatigable efforts to secure loans and her painstaking scholarship are reflected in the selection of works displayed and in her illuminating essay. Our particular appreciation is expressed as well to Carmen Martinez and Viviane Grimminger, holders of the González Estate in Paris, who contributed not only many important works but infinite time, energy and devoted attention to all stages of the exhibition's organization.

The Musée National d'Art Moderne, Centre Georges Pompidou, Paris, as the institution with the largest collection of González's original sculptures, deserves special thanks for its generous loans, as do the Museo de Arte Moderno, Barcelona, and the Museo Español de Arte Contemporáneo, Madrid, for their significant contributions. And we must also express our indebtedness to all the other participating institutions and collections for their generosity and understanding in parting with unique and irreplaceable works of art. For help in securing and documenting loans we are grateful to the following individuals: E. Baud and A. Ginisty, Paris and Vézelay; Michèle Cantinaud and Catherine Thieck, Yves de Fontbrune, Marwan Hoss and Jacques Vilian, Paris; David Grob, London; Arnold Glimcher and Jeffrey Hoffeld, New York.

The pursuit of research on an artist as little documented as González has not been a simple task. All scholars are indebted to their predecessors, and in this regard we must express our debt to Josephine Withers for her monograph on González, which represents a serious early attempt to identify and establish a catalogue of sculptures. We are also grateful to Jörn Merkert, Director of the Visual Arts Section of the Akademie der Künste, Berlin, and author of the forthcoming catalogue raisonné of the sculptures, for long hours of discussions that clarified sequence, titles and dates. We must here express our appreciation to the following persons for information and documentation on González, the man and the artist, his contacts during his lifetime and his materials, technique and process: Sergi Aguilar, Barcelona; Pierrette Gargallo-Anguera, Paris; Henri Goetz, Paris; Hans Hartung, Antibes; Susi Magnelli, Meudon; Cora Rosevear, New York; Hélène Seckel, Paris; and Augusto Torres, Montevideo and Barcelona.

All museum exhibitions reflect the combined efforts of a devoted professional staff, and in this context we would like to thank Deborah Leveton and Elizabeth Brown for their extreme diligence as Curatorial Assistants on this project, Carol Fuerstein for editing the extensive catalogue; Saul Fuerstein for the preparation of the works for presentation, Harold B. Nelson for accomplishing the difficult task of assembling the exhibition and Scott Wixon for a particularly complex installation.

It is impossible to mount exhibitions of ambitious scope without generous financial assistance. The present undertaking is no exception and could not have been realized without the aid of the National Endowment for the Arts; the Spain–U.S. Joint Committee for Educational and Cultural Affairs; the Cultural Department of the Ministry of Foreign Affairs of Spain; and the Arthur Ross Foundation. We express our sincere gratitude for their enlightened support.

THOMAS M. MESSER, *Director*
The Solomon R. Guggenheim Foundation

Paris, ca. 1900-02

I have just returned from New York, and the beautiful exhibition of your father's work. The Museum has installed the exhibition expensively and tastefully. It really looks beautiful. The artists of New York and there are many, have all expressed admiration and enthusiasm. But, there are a dozen of us who have always recognized the genius and beauty, the innovation, of González since 1930.[1]

I have loaned the photo of your father's studio . . . to my friend, the sculptor Theodore Roszak, who is writing a section on new sculpture for the Encyclopedia Brittanica. . . . I presume he will record González as the father of all iron sculpture of this century.[2]

David Smith to Roberta González, 1956

Ca. 1937

JULIO GONZALEZ: TECHNIQUE, SYNTAX, CONTEXT

MARGIT ROWELL

1. Letter dated February 28, 1956, from David Smith to Julio González's daughter Roberta, on the occasion of the González retrospective at The Museum of Modern Art, New York. González Estate Archive, Paris. The author is indebted to Carmen Martinez and Viviane Grimminger for making this material available.

2. Letter dated June 11, 1956, from David Smith to Roberta González. González Estate Archive, Paris.

3. According to Dorothy Dehner, Smith's first wife, Smith first saw works by González reproduced in magazines, which Graham brought back from Europe, but she is unsure of the exact publication references. Smith apparently asked, "How does he make them?" to which Graham replied, "They are welded." Subsequently Smith saw the three works by González that Graham had purchased in Paris. The author is indebted to Dorothy Dehner for this account and further insights into Smith's relationship to González in the 1930s. (Interview with the author, New York, November 15, 1982.)

4. The earliest reproductions of Picasso's metal sculptures from this period appeared in the Surrealist publication *Minotaure*, no. 1, 1933, pp. 9-29 (photographs by Brassaï).

5. *David Smith by David Smith*, ed. Cleve Gray, New York, Chicago, San Francisco, 1968, p. 25.

6. González's term was *"dessiner dans l'espace"*

In the early 1930s the American artist David Smith discovered the metal sculptures of Julio González in the collection of his friend John Graham.[3] According to Smith, the adaptation of the common skills of metalworking to the art of making sculpture was a revelation. Smith himself had worked as a welder in an automobile plant. Earlier he had studied painting. But upon his discovery of González's sculptures, as well as the sculptures by Picasso made in collaboration with González between 1928 and 1931 (which he saw in reproduction)[4] Smith was encouraged to orient his activity toward the creation of forged- and welded-metal sculpture.

Like all artists of his generation, Smith was impressed by Picasso's genius in the creation of unprecedented images. But, in contrast to his peers, his personal experience in industrial metalwork singularly disposed him to understand the nature of González's contribution in the execution of Picasso's sculptures and in his independent work. In Smith's own words, "I saw a chance to make sculpture in a tradition I was already rooted in."[5] In 1933 Smith produced his first group of forged sculptures, one of which was inspired directly by a work by González in John Graham's collection (see cat. no. 88). And at the end of the year he bought his first oxyacetylyne welding torch.

One of the few artists to have early acknowledged González's importance in the development of a welded-metal idiom for sculpture, Smith perceived in him a sensibility and background much like his own. Like González, Smith had no academic training as a sculptor. In consonance with the general climate in America at that time, he respected González as a simple working man, whose aesthetic evolved from artisanal fabrication techniques. He admired the Catalan sculptor's raw economical art because it reflected a knowledge of the singular qualities and methods of working metal. Smith understood that only a man with González's experience in direct-metal processes could reduce the accepted concept of sculpture in the twentieth century to a kind of planar, linear essence, what González termed "to draw in space."[6]

Smith's understanding that González's process of making determined his formal interpretations probably contributed to his own "new concept process," which he defined as follows:

That is where the distant whole or finished work consists of the sum of its parts. This is much like the industrial method of building a machine but without a blueprint, and where the function is only visual. Where the end is never seen until the final part, and the finality being realized when each part in unity works up to the whole. Conceptually this procedure is much like painting. The sculptural entity never takes place until summed up by its parts.

Romantically speaking, the indication of form by bulk mass does not possess its old validity. Mass is energy. Space is energy. Nothing is without energy. Nothing is without mass. The indication of area or pattern is a statement of energy and as sculptural as sculpture can be....[7]

At the same time, this is one of the most accurate descriptions of González's process and art.

Although González is generally cited as the father of modern metal sculpture, his name is usually overshadowed by those of Picasso and David Smith. González did not have an eventful life-story. His mature career was short, his personality was retiring and the scale of his production—in both size and number of the pieces—was modest. At the beginning, in his artisanal work, his materials and technique—those of the wrought-iron trade— were classical and traditional. But by the time he died in 1942 at the age of sixty-six, he had laid the foundations of the modern idiom of abstract welded-metal sculpture.

Up to the 1930s, when González made his breakthrough, almost all sculpture was carved or modeled.[8] Metal was used only in casting. Few, if any, artists looked toward forged or welded metal as a possible medium for their work, primarily because it did not correspond to their conception of sculptural images. Moreover, unlike casting, executed by expert technicians in a foundry, the direct working of metal demanded an active intervention of the artist's hand, which in itself required a long and specialized apprenticeship.

González received his early professional training as a decorative metalsmith. Decorative metalworking is a craft based on steady, accurate draftsmanship, an intimate knowledge of the specifications of different metals, and a training in the techniques of their shaping, forging and finishing: cutting, heating, hammering, soldering and polishing. The decorative metalsmith's basic medium is the metal sheet or strip, which, incidentally, is relatively inappropriate to sculpture in the round. He is called upon to create objects for general consumption, according to prescribed stylistic canons. The products of this trade are usually flat or linear, designed to fill a given space and a precise ornamental function. One might thus presume that González's background would not predispose him to transgress the conventions of twentieth-century sculpture. Yet it is precisely his formation in the applied arts and his specific lack of training in the "fine art" of sculpture that would engender his singular process, and ultimately his vision.

Biographical data on González is spare. There are few monographs on the artist and relatively little reliable documentation.[9] Moreover, few of González's acquaintances survive to supplement this material.[10] Furthermore, myth and legend converge to portray the man as modest, religious, devoted to his work and family and loathe to participate in any social activity, even the modest café life of his colleagues.

It appears to be fact rather than mere myth that González devoted the greater part of his existence to his family and his work. His family consisted of his mother (until her death in 1928), his two older sisters Pilar and Lola (both of whom outlived him), his daughter Roberta and his companion Marie-Thérèse whom he married in 1937. As the only male member of this Catalan household, González felt morally responsible for their economic subsistence. In reality, however, everyone in the family contributed to the humble but adequate revenues. His two sisters, who had been successful dressmakers in Barcelona, continued this activity in Paris, supplementing it with the sale of laces and embroideries. Marie-Thérèse, also in the fashion world, generated commissions for accessories such as jewelry, buttons, buckles, most of which were made by Julio in his metal workshop. In the early years González had antiques sent from Spain and sold them in Paris. In the late teens the family had a shop on the boulevard Raspail where it sold laces, antiques and González's handcrafted jewelry and decorative objects. Although it did not keep the store throughout González's lifetime, the family continued to receive commissions from the fashion industry until the artist's death.[11]

These details of the artist's biography are significant in that they shed some light on his mentality. González never attempted to earn a living from his sculpture. On the contrary, he sought to subsidize his art through other activities in order to retain complete freedom and not subject it to commercial considerations. As a Catalan, he was a proud, private and religious man. His Catholicism notwithstanding, González's work was his religion and few were admitted to the sanctuary of his studio. Most collectors and critics were turned away, the exceptions being close and long-standing friends such as Maurice Raynal, Alexandre Mercereau, André Salmon, Christian Zervos. To others González maintained he had nothing to show. Small wonder that during his lifetime he sold very little.

This deliberate isolation does not mean that González was naive or unaware of the art going on around him. Although self-taught,

in his text "Picasso sculpteur et les cathédrales," published in Josephine Withers, *Julio Gonzalez: Sculpture in Iron*, New York, 1978, Appendix I, p. 141. This passage refers to González's ideal of sculpture in general.

7. *David Smith by David Smith*, p. 54.

8. For exceptions to this premise see Margit Rowell, *The Planar Dimension: Europe, 1912-1932*, exh. cat. New York, The Solomon R. Guggenheim Museum, 1979.

9. We have traced seven monographs on the artist (see bibliography), exclusive of exhibition catalogues. With the exception of the Merkert catalogue raisonné, these were compiled primarily from the family archives and recollections and therefore, understandably, lack precision in certain areas.

10. The author is grateful to Henri Goetz, Paris; Hans Hartung, Antibes; Susi Magnelli, Meudon; and Augusto Torres, Montevideo and Barcelona, for firsthand information on González.

11. This information on the family's activities in antiques and fashion has been gleaned from papers in the González Estate Archive, Paris. Letters dated 1936 and 1940 mention continuing orders for buttons from Paris couture houses.

Front row: left to right, Pilar, Lola, González, Barcelona, 1890-92

González with his sisters, Pilar and Lola, and unidentified friend, probably in Mme Ricou's apartment, Paris, ca. 1915-18. Note Brancusi sculpture on mantlepiece

12. Henri Goetz (interview with the author, Paris, January 8, 1982) insisted that this was so. See, by contrast, William Tucker's otherwise excellent *The Language of Sculpture*, London, 1974, in which he unfortunately perpetuates the conventional image of González as without ambition or means to work in other mediums (p. 76).

13. In Withers, *Gonzalez*, English transl., p. 135. (N.b. The author has made a few minor corrections in Withers's translations.)

14. Joan, who was eight years older than Julio, died tragically in 1908.

he was cultivated, loved to read, listen to music and visit medieval monuments. He had many friends in the Spanish (mostly Catalan) community in Paris: Picasso, Manolo, Paco Durrio, Pablo Gargallo, Joaquín Torres-García, whom he saw regularly and with whom he exhibited. Alberto Magnelli and Constantin Brancusi were also his friends.

Yet González chose to make his way alone. Not quite as modest as his legend would portray him, he was convinced of his own genius. He was also convinced that forged metal was the future language of sculpture and he used it from choice, not from necessity.[12] His often quoted statement reflects this belief: "The age of iron began many centuries ago, by producing (unhappily) arms—some very beautiful. Today it makes possible the building of bridges, railroads. It is high time that this metal cease to be a murderer and the simple instrument of an overly mechanical science. Today, the door is opened wide to this material to be at last ! forged and hammered by the peaceful hands of artists."[13]

In order to situate González's oeuvre and define his particular contribution to twentieth-century sculpture, a word must be said about his training and background. González came from a line of Barcelona metalsmiths that went back at least to his paternal grandfather. By the age of fifteen he was apprenticed in his father's workshop. Here, along with his older brother Joan,[14] he learned to cut, hammer and forge all types of metals, executing decorative objects and jewelry in a late nineteenth century style. The products of the González workshop were renowned in Barcelona and won prizes in national and international exhibitions. In the evenings Joan and Julio studied drawing at the Escuela des Bellas Artes. This was probably acceptable to their father because drawing is fundamental to the applied-art professions. Before moving to Paris in 1900, the two brothers frequented the avant-garde milieu of the café Els Quatre Gats. Despite the aspiration of

fig. 3
Gargallo
Large Harlequin (Harlequin Playing a Flute). 1931
Bronze, 38⅝" (98 cm.) high
Collection Musée National d'Art Moderne, Centre
Georges Pompidou, Paris

since 1928 (see pp. 19-27 here). Gargallo used metal to enact a figurative vision. The result suggests the presence of full curvilinear, naturalistic (although somewhat caricatural) volumes. His lines are even, fluid: a perfect penman's draft. His planes are hammered smooth. His sculptures are first a specific referential image, and only secondly of metal. By contrast, González's *Harlequin* is first a medium—iron in its rawest state, in flat sheets and bars—and only secondly an image. Some lines are awkwardly forged, some contours are ragged, calling attention to material and process. His spaces, inscribed by line and plane, are not descriptive. The sculpture constitutes a reality of its own. It refers to nothing else.

As has been mentioned, in the early years González aspired to be a painter. Yet from the beginning it is clear that he had more talent as a draftsman. His paintings, executed in a flat fresco style with emphasis on masses, are interesting in their initiation of themes he would develop throughout his lifetime (Woman Combing Her Hair, Maternity), and in their stylistic references to Puvis de Chavannes or affinities with Picasso and the Barcelona school (cat. nos. 5-8). Yet they never showed a strong painterly personality. His drawings are a startling confirmation of the uniformity of the turn-of-the-century School of Barcelona style. Practically indistinguishable from drawings by Picasso, Ramón Casas or other members of the Els Quatre Gats group, they reveal a natural graphic facility. Early examples of González's prizewinning metalwork—forged-metal flowers, jewelry, repoussé masks and portraits—exhibit the skills of a consummate craftsman. Indeed, until the late 1920s González had no ambition to be a sculptor. It is said that not until he was approached by Picasso to help execute ideas for metal sculptures did the meaning and possibilities of the world of sculpture open to him.

17. A text by González was published in *Cahiers d'Art*, vol. 12, no. 6-7, 1937, p. 189, in which he refers specifically to Picasso's Cubist constructions.

18. See Josephine Withers, "The Artistic Collaboration of Pablo Picasso and Julio González," *Art Journal*, vol. XXXV, Winter 1975-76, p. 109.

19. Christian Zervos, *Picasso: Oeuvres*, Paris, 1955, vol. VII, p. 62, fig. 140; Werner Spies, *Sculpture by Picasso*, New York, 1971, pp. 72-73, repr.

20. According to Alexandre Istrati and Natalia Dumitresco (interview with the author, Paris, March 17, 1982), González worked for his friend Brancusi, probably as early as 1925-26, when Brancusi was preparing his 1926 exhibition at the Brummer Gallery, New York. They maintain that Brancusi "always had studio assistants." At the time González was a metalsmith aspiring to be a painter. The same sources assert "Brancusi would not have hired a sculptor." Conceivably González built the metal armatures for Brancusi's plaster models and may have helped polish some of the metal sculptures. According to Augusto Torres (interview with the author, New York,

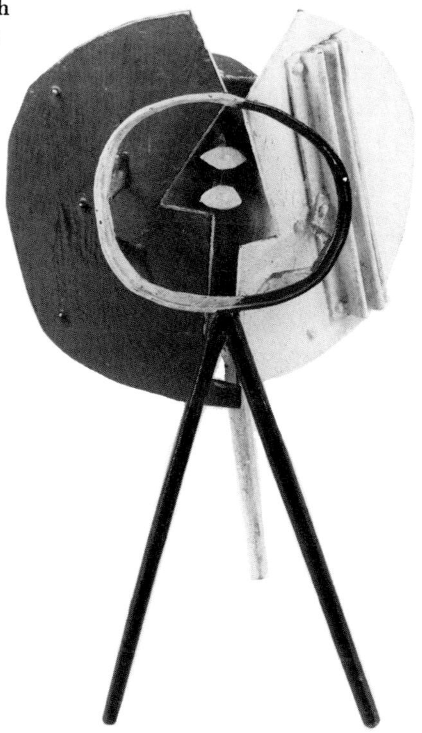

April 16, 1982), González
was a superb technician
and rigorous perfection-
ist: when he taught
Torres to polish metal,
he said it had to shine
like the back of a pocket
watch. In May 1928,
upon his mother's death,
González wrote to Bran-
cusi and Picasso that he
was having financial dif-
ficulties and that if they
intended to use his ser-
vices in the future, he
needed some money in
advance. (González letter
to Brancusi in possession
of Istrati and Dumitresco,
Paris; Picasso reply to
presumably identical let-
ter in González Estate Archive, Paris.)

A large stylized forged-
metal kettle hook and a
spinning rod in the
Brancusi estate are tra-
ditionally dated 1928.
Attributed to Brancusi,
one wonders if they
might not be the fruit of,
at the very least, a collaboration between him and
González, since we know
of no other forged iron-
work by Brancusi's hand.
González continued to
frequent Brancusi's stu-
dio at least until 1930, indicated by a sketch,
surely done from sight
rather than memory, rep-
resenting Brancusi's *Bird
in Space,* found in one of
González's notebooks;
the notebook contains
González's preliminary
notes dated 1930 for his
text on Picasso.

Between 1928 and 1931 González assisted
Picasso in the execution of six metal sculptures. This collaboration is documented in
both the Picasso and González literature. Although it is usually stated that Picasso had a
major influence on González as a result of this
close working relationship, the exact measure
of their exchange in the areas of iconographical motifs, process and vision has not been
fully explored. Beyond any doubt, the work
with Picasso changed the direction of González's entire career. Yet during the first years
of this collaboration (1928-29), there is no
sign of its impact except that González began
making less decorative pieces, indicating that
he was exploring a more autonomous creative
mode.

González's first experimental works that
show an attempt to move away from his traditional training in hammered metal and conventional ornamental imagery were executed
in 1929 (see cat. nos. 65, 73). They may be
defined according to their process, as drawings on sheets of metal in which the contours
were incised with a jeweler's saw and the
planes pushed forward and back in depth,
creating zones of light and lines of shadow.
Unlike Picasso's Cubist constructions of
1912-18, which González knew,[17] these pieces
are not pictorial assemblages based on color,
texture and a complex layering of planes.
They are simpler: drawings where the pencil
has been replaced by the saw. In some works
of 1929, such as *Still Life II* (cat. no. 74), he
even cut out and discarded certain areas, then
added new planes in relief; in others he broke
apart the image according to his draftsman's
logic and superimposed separate lit and
shaded planes (see cat. nos. 67, 68, 70). The
visible soldering or riveting indicates that
there was no attempt to conceal technique.

González's basic medium was the metal
plate or sheet, combined with strips and rods
of different shapes and sizes. Whether copper,
iron, brass or bronze, these were the common
materials of the metalsmith's trade, which
González knew how to procure and work. Despite a few early attempts to make sculpture

in the round (cat. nos. 39, 56-58), it seems
not to have occurred to González at this stage
to make three-dimensional works shaped from
the mass. Clearly the techniques of his pro-
fession, known since childhood, influenced his
vision and direction.

The works of 1929-30 cited above were produced during the first stages of the Picasso-
González collaboration. Apparently, the first
piece the artists made together was Picasso's
small *Head* of 1928 (fig. 4).[18] Preliminary
drawings for it are dated March 20, 1928,
and Werner Spies asserts that Picasso con-
tacted González at that time and asked him to
help him make metal sculpture.[19] For the
sheet-metal sculpture he had in mind, Picasso
had neither the equipment nor the technique.
González had both. Furthermore, he had been
a family friend of Picasso since childhood and
was an artist of modest means who willingly
provided technical assistance to Brancusi and
other artists in order to supplement his income.[20] Presumably the piece was made that
spring.

This *Head,* despite its modest dimensions,
would have a major influence on the first and
one of the most abstract pieces González
would make in 1930: *The Kiss* (cat. no. 109).
It would take him two years and a working

fig. 5
Picasso
Wire Construction. 1928-29
Iron, 19⅞″ (50.5 cm.) high
Collection Musée Picasso, Paris

through of other cutout heads and motifs to arrive at what can be seen as a reinterpretation of Picasso's sculpture. Reciprocally, the drawings related to González's sculpture (cat. nos. 107, 108) help us decipher Picasso's *Head* as two interlocking profiles, one positive, one negative, one male, one female. It is a kiss. A notebook of Picasso of June 1928 contains sketches of the kiss motif;[21] and the same theme is found in paintings of 1929 and 1931.[22]

González's drawings show clearer links with his visual sources than do his final sculptures. For particularly complex or ambitious sculptures, González sometimes worked out his concept on paper, devising a variety of solutions. Yet almost always when he began to work with his metal medium, he improvised in space. Sculpture was not the mere execution of a predesigned idea for him. Quite literally it was a drawing in space. In this particular instance, some of the drawings show superimposed linear (wire) and planar oval motifs and tentative solutions for a wire stand. These may also derive from Picasso's original concept.[23]

Picasso's wire constructions of 1928-29 mark the next stage of the two artists' collaboration (fig. 5). In August of 1928, while vacationing at Dinard in Brittany, Picasso made over a dozen line drawings inspired by bathers at the beach.[24] These sketches show the various linear configurations that Picasso intended as wire sculptures, which would be executed upon his return to Paris. According to Spies, González may have executed one or more of these modest-scale models singlehandedly, following Picasso's drawings. And indeed, in some of them the smooth angles, cleanly soldered joints and hammered extremities reflect a master craftsman's skills.[25]

González probably looked back to these linear constructions when he undertook his own strictly linear pieces in 1934-35. However, by this time his vision and technique had evolved far beyond the fairly elementary structures executed for Picasso. Picasso's concept was undeniably revolutionary, and probably with-

21. Carnet 21, Collection Marina Picasso. See *Pablo Picasso: Sammlung Marina Picasso*, exh. cat., Munich, Haus der Kunst, p. 134, repr.

22. For example, *Le Baiser*, August 25, 1929, and *Le Baiser*, January 12, 1931, Collection Musée Picasso, Paris. *Picasso, Oeuvres reçues en paiement des droits de succession*, exh. cat., Paris, Grand Palais, 1980, p. 138, no. 170, and p. 144, no. 190, repr.

23. Sidney Geist has suggested that González may have been inspired by Brancusi's recurrent theme of *The Kiss* (Geist, *Brancusi/The Kiss*, New York, 1978, p. 91). Although González certainly knew these works, the formal analogies with Picasso's imagery are more convincing.

24. Carnet 1044, Collection Marina Picasso. *Sammlung Marina Picasso*, pp. 145-148, repr.

25. See Spies in *Sammlung Marina Picasso*, pp. 317, 318.

Alan Bowness indicates that at least one of these original constructions

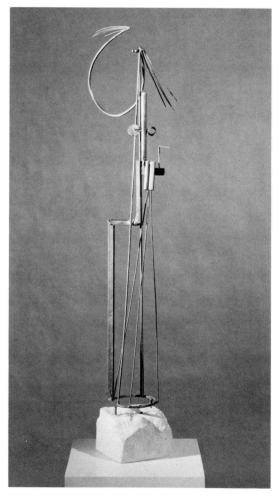

fig. 6
Julio González
Maternity. ca. 1934
Iron, 51¾″ (130.5 cm.) high
Collection The Trustees of the Tate Gallery, London

fig. 7
Picasso
Woman in the Garden. 1929-30
Painted iron, 81⅛″ (206 cm.) high
Collection Musée Picasso, Paris

may be dated October 1928, as published in *Cahiers d'Art*, vol. IV, January 1929, p. 6. See Bowness, "Picasso's Sculpture," in *Picasso in Retrospect*, New York, 1973, reprinted 1980, p. 191, fn. 22.

Three of the original wire models belong to the Musée Picasso, Paris. See *Picasso, Oeuvres reçues en paiement*, p. 132, no. 161, and p. 134, nos. 162 and 163, repr. A larger version of no. 161, executed somewhat later, is in the Collection Marina Picasso, see Ibid., pp. 316-317, repr. (Dimensions should read 95 x 86 x 79 cm.) A further enlargement supervised by Picasso and measuring almost two meters high (including steel base) was loaned to The Museum of Modern Art, New York (where it has now entered the collection), with Picasso's authorization to execute a monumental enlargement measuring almost four meters high (including base). This version was completed in Cor-ten steel in 1972; it is usually on view in the Museum's sculpture garden. The author is grateful to Hélène Seckel, Musée Picasso, Paris, and Cora Rosevear, The Museum of Modern Art, New York, for clarification of some of these points.

26. Spies, in *Sammlung Marina Picasso*, p. 318.

27. In Withers, *Gonzalez*, p. 142, English transl. p. 135.

out it González would not have developed sculptures in the same vein; but Picasso conceived his sculptures in the form of drawings, which were executed exactly to specifications by a master craftsman. González's works of 1934—the Tate *Maternity* (fig. 6), the Stockholm *Woman Combing Her Hair*, the Maeght Foundation *Large Standing Figure* (cat. nos. 149, 154), for example—represent an elaborate intepretive and structural syntax. They illustrate the vision, logic and skills of a man who thinks, sees and assembles directly in metal.

Picasso's *Woman in the Garden*, 1929-30 (fig. 7), the third product of the collaboration, does not manifest the technical perfection that characterized the wire constructions painstakingly executed by González. Picasso maintained to Spies that he assembled this piece himself, thus accounting for the awkwardness and "authenticity" of its execution.[26] González, in a manuscript on Picasso, which he started the year this piece was finished, also suggests that this was so:

Picasso never finds the time to execute one of his projects. If, rarely, he makes up his mind, he settles on his most recent idea. For he is so restless, always wanting to improve, he only succeeds in filling new pages of his sketchbook. This is why, in spite of the thousands of studies, he took not a one the morning of the day he went to work at the forge; his hammer alone was enough to try to execute his monument to Apollinaire. He worked on it for several months and he finished it. He would often say, "Once again I feel as happy as I was in 1912."[27]

It seems plausible that González was referring in this text to his own working methods: a preparation of images through drawings, but ultimately a free improvisation in space.

The *Woman in the Garden*, one of the projects originally proposed as a monument to Apollinaire, is a complex piece. Inspired by Picasso's paintings of the late 1920s, it is a linear skeleton, rhythmically punctuated by flat or curved planes. The linear elements are made of scrap metal (sectional bars, wire, nails, probably collected in González's studio), which produces a syncopated discontinuity. Similarly, the bulbous shape in the lower part of the woman's figure is an unidentified found object. The other planar motifs, which derive from Picasso's familiar iconography, were probably drawn on the plates by Picasso and cut out by González. The cup-shaped head (behind the flat facial plane) was forged, we may assume, by González. It is thus probable that González prepared the components of the sculpture to Picasso's specifications, and Picasso assembled them.

Picasso told Spies he was unhappy his sculpture could not be placed out-of-doors because it was sheet iron and would rust.[28] Therefore, in 1930 he commissioned González to make a replica—not by casting but by cutting and assembling bronze components and mounting the piece to scale. Augusto Torres, Torres-García's eldest son, reports that as he was learning metalwork in González's studio at that time, he helped to cut and polish the elements of the replica. According to his account, Picasso regularly visited the studio on the rue Médéah to view the work in progress, but González executed the sculpture alone.[29] The bronze was subsequently placed in Picasso's garden at Boisgeloup.[30]

The *Woman in the Garden* was an important piece, not only for Picasso but for González. It was Picasso's first large-scale sculpture closely related to his painting and the first in which he allowed the random principle to play a part. The found elements, as opposed to the carefully cut sections, brought a new and unexpected expressivity to Picasso's art, and he would exploit this factor of incongruity in much of his sculpture in later years. González, on the other hand, discovered the assemblage principle and the potential force of combining disparate parts. He observed the rhythmic discontinuity obtained by assembling diverse linear segments in a single graphic line. He learned the evocative power of images distilled into skeletal lines and planes. And in forging the replica, he

learned to create motifs of an entirely unaccustomed type, translating found objects into handmade, arbitrary shapes.

During the period between 1930 and 1932 Picasso and González worked on three more metal sculptures: *Figure of a Woman, Head,* and *Head of a Woman* (figs. 8, 9, 10). In each the improvised assemblage principle became more explicit, coupled with an almost exclusive use of scrap metal. From now until 1931 any cutout, welded or shaped motifs in Picasso's sculpture would be limited to the most elementary forms: circles, ovals, squares, cones.

Picasso's *Figure of a Woman* and *Head,* both of 1930, evolved from sketches made in August and November 1928.[31] The drawings show that *Figure of a Woman* was not originally conceived as a sculpture in metal. However, perhaps the artist's recent experience of working with González combined with his discovery of a shoemaker's metal last were what changed its destiny. Other sketches indicate that *Head* was originally projected as the head for a standing figure, comparable to the wire constructions of 1928-29. Once again the basic morphology originates in Picasso's paintings executed after 1926. But now Picasso was concentrating on sculpture and it is plausible that he turned also to the sculpture he favored most: African masks and figurines. Some of the sketches for the isolated *Head* have a definite African feeling, which is maintained in the sculpture.[32] For example, the superposition of a lozenge shape over a rectangle is a traditional Ibo motif, as is the conic neck. Pursuing this line of inquiry, one might compare the elongated proportions of the *Figure of a Woman* as it was finally realized—particularly in the tiny head and long neck—to Dogon or Senufo figurines. This is not to say that Picasso was trying to reproduce African models, but that his familiarity with African art made certain motifs and proportions acceptable. The same considerations apply to the tiny head with three closely set punctures denoting eyes and mouth, a facial schema common to Ivory Coast masks.

28. The author learned this information from Arnold Glimcher, New York, who received it verbally from Spies. Picasso appears to have expressed his sentiments to González as well. See Ibid.

29. Interview with the author, New York, April 16, 1982. To our knowledge, this is the first time the actual method of fabrication of this bronze replica has been clarified and published. All earlier authors seem to have assumed it was a cast. Yet a close study of the piece (in the Collection Marina Picasso, see *Sammlung Marina Picasso*, pp. 318-319, repr.), together with Torres's testimony, proves without a doubt that it is a forged bronze. Both the iron and the bronze were exhibited at the Galerie Georges Petit, Paris, June 16–July 30, 1932, cat. nos. 229 and 230 respectively.

30. See Brassaï, *Conversations with Picasso*, Paris, 1964, p. 33, where Brassaï tells of his visit to Boisgeloup in December 1932 and his discovery of *Woman in the Garden* in Picasso's garden. Unfortunately, he refers to the sculpture as *The Stag (Le Cerf)* (no sculpture of this name exists) and assumes it was in iron, when in fact it was the bronze version of *Woman in the Garden*.

31. Carnet 1044, Collection Marina Picasso. *Sammlung Marina Picasso*, pp. 141-155, repr.

32. Ibid., p. 155, repr.

fig. 8
Picasso
Figure of a Woman. 1930
Iron, 31⅞″ (81 cm.) high
Collection Maya Widmaier, Marseilles

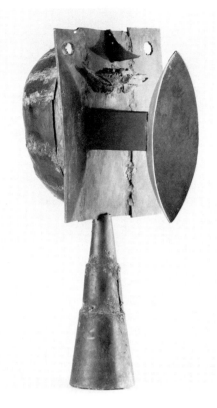

fig. 9
Picasso
Head. 1930
Iron, brass and bronze, 32⅞″ (83.5 cm.) high
Collection Musée Picasso, Paris

fig. 10
Picasso
Head of a Woman. 1931
Painted iron, sheet metal and found objects, 39⅜″
(100 cm.) high
Collection Musée Picasso, Paris

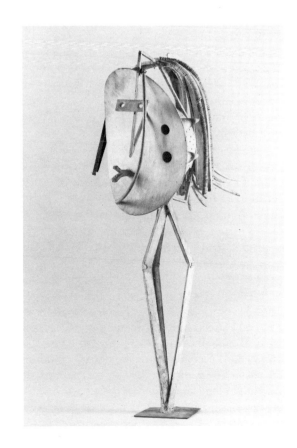

If Picasso was looking at African art at this time, this would explain certain obvious but unprecedented parallel references in the work of González during the years 1930-31. Unquestionably, the *Masque "My"* (cat. no. 82) and the *Head in Polished Iron* (fig. 11) and their related drawings (cat. nos. 81, 83) allude to African models. Their austerely schematic and chiseled features set them apart from the rest of the artist's production of that time.

Head of a Woman of 1931 is the final metal sculpture of the collaboration of the artist and the metalsmith. It is altogether the most surprising and completely resolved image to emerge from their hands. Although we know of no sketches precisely relating to this sculpture and the exact constitution of its components would develop during the act of making, Picasso presumably had a clear idea of the configuration he wanted. Werner Spies reports: "He told me that it suddenly occurred to him to construct the back of the head out of colanders. 'I said to González, go and get some colanders. And he brought back two brand-new ones.'"[33] The device of a cup-shaped head behind a frontal plane indicating a face had been used already in the *Woman in the Garden*, although the feeling and cutout facial silhouette are quite different there. As we recall, González probably forged that shape in the earlier piece. This time Picasso wanted a more provocative, aleatory solution.

Whether Picasso was inspired by Kota reliquary figures in the composition of his image we do not know. Yet the proportions of parts to whole, the slightly concave oval of the face, the tightly coiled wire bedsprings of the hair and the splaying of the neck into a lozenge shape bring these singular metal silhouettes to mind. Picasso had seen Kota reliquaries in his pre-Cubist days, and the effects are visible in his "Dancing Figures" of 1907.[34] As for the projecting mouth, a projecting orifice—eye or mouth—is characteristic of many kinds of African masks.

Like the iron *Woman in the Garden*, *Head of a Woman* was painted white, which unifies

fig. 11
González
Head in Polished Iron. ca. 1930
Iron, 10⅝″ (27 cm.) high
Ex. collection Alex Maguy, Paris

its parts, softens its raw brutality and betrays its pictorial source in the linear silhouettes on white grounds seen in the Studio paintings of 1926-29 (fig. 12). The linear wire profile that passes in front of the curved facial plane echoes the multiplied facial contours or skeletal lines used in the same paintings.

The complexity of this piece and its seamless execution suggest that once again González effected the welding and soldering following Picasso's instructions. Assuming that Picasso did indeed assemble it, the *Woman in the Garden* may be the unique sculpture of this period that he put together himself. In the subsequent pieces Picasso's expressivity was achieved through the disparity of parts rather than through a relatively awkward technique. This was consonant with an emphasis on imagery, characteristic of a painter's sensibility. So that these sculptures, more aggressive and provocative in their morphological components, required an invisible and effortless technique.

As has been suggested, González learned a great deal from this collaboration with Picasso, and it is interesting to see how a num-

33. Spies, *Sculpture by Picasso*, p. 75. It has sometimes been suggested that this piece was made in Boisgeloup. However it is known that González did not drive a car and thus to "go and get some colanders" would have been a major undertaking involving a chauffeur. This seems to favor the thesis that *Head of a Woman*, like the other collaborative sculptures, was executed in González's studio on the rue Médéah.

34. For example, *Nude with Raised Arms (The Dancer of Avignon)*, 1907, Private Collection, New York. *Pablo Picasso*, ed. William Rubin, exh. cat., New York, The Museum of Modern Art, 1980, pp. 100-101, repr.

fig. 12
Picasso
Woman with Palette and Easel. 1928
Oil on canvas, 51¼ x 38¼″ (130 x 97 cm.)
Collection Musée Picasso, Paris

ber of specific motifs initiated by Picasso recur, sometimes with surprising constancy, in González's sculptures throughout the years. In some cases the primary attribution of motifs to Picasso is unquestionable, since they originate in paintings completed earlier than the sculptures. For other compositional arrangements, found in the work of both men, it is more difficult to establish primacy, and perhaps this is relatively unimportant. Since the artists were working side by side in the same metal studio, that they shared or borrowed images would appear quite normal, particularly since many motifs and compositional devices were dictated by the materials and generated by the very process of making metal sculpture.

For example, the lock-of-hair motif at the upper right of Picasso's 1928 *Head* (fig. 4) will occur with frequency throughout González's production of 1929-31. Picasso's hair motif, seen in paintings as early as 1927 (fig. 12) but absent from the initial drawings for this sculpture, is a length of corrugated metal, which one might guess he found lying in the metalsmith's studio. In his sculptures he would not repeat this motif exactly, whereas González would use this same shorthand sign—identical in reductiveness and slant—in many heads of 1929-30 (see cat. nos. 66, 67, 82). Moreover, it appears explicitly in the drawings for *The Kiss* as well as in the final sculpture (cat. nos. 107-109).

Again, motifs and compositional devices seen in Picasso's *Woman in the Garden* are present in González's sculptures in 1930 and after. The structuring of the head as an open cup-shape, partially covered by cutout facial planes is common in González's pieces of 1930 and 1931. The closest examples include the *Little Peasant Woman* and *The Lovers !* and *II* (cat. nos. 95, 122, 123), although there are other, looser interpretations. Picasso's cutout facial silhouette was anguished and distorted, analogous to those in his paintings of the same period. Although González experimented with stylized cut and layered planes in early masks of 1929, these obeyed formal rather than ex-

fig. 13
Picasso
Nude on White Ground. 1928
Oil on canvas, 51¼ x 38⅝″ (130 x 98 cm.)
Collection Musée Picasso, Paris

pressive objectives. Subsequently, he would elaborate on Picasso's tipped, triangulated silhouette as a negative shape in the *Lovers I* and *II*, for example. Thereafter this acutely stylized and distorted head reappears periodically in González's oeuvre in different forms and interpretations, as in the *Small Sickle (Figure of a Woman)* of 1936 (cat. no. 204) and the slightly later *Monsieur Cactus* and *Madame Cactus* (cat. nos. 226, 233). Once again the drawings are more revealing of the visual sources than the sculptures (cat. nos. 203, 220, 229-231). The flying locks of hair also apparent in Picasso's paintings of 1928-29 will be a common motif throughout González's production, although in personalized formal variations. The nose in Picasso's *Woman in the Garden,* a curved plane set perpendicular to the face, is repeated in *Head in Depth* (cat. no. 104), one of González's few dated sculptures from 1930. The roughly cut and assembled planes of the neck of this and other heads of the 1930 period also echo Picasso's *Woman in the Garden.*

The fact that Picasso may have invented certain visual concepts that González would continue to elaborate long after Picasso had abandoned them does not necessarily diminish González's stature. In most instances here, Picasso's visual ideas evolved from his paintings. And with no metalwork training and no preconceived ideas about the limits of metal sculpture, he was freer to improvise. González was less mature in his vision as an artist. But his understanding of metal and its techniques produced a heightened awareness of the iconographical potentials he discovered. By working on Picasso's sculptures, González immersed himself in a world of basic forms and processes he could assimilate to his emerging syntax and develop throughout the ensuing years.

In many ways the *Harlequin* (cat. no. 112) is a summing up of González's experience with Picasso, a kind of homage to his friend. As Josephine Withers has pointed out, the morphology of this sculpture has much to do with Picasso's paintings of 1926-30 on the Harle-

quin theme and relates in particular to a canvas by that name of March 1930 that González must have known.[35] But Picasso's treatment of the theme, unlike González's, was strictly two dimensional. González's sculpture, executed the final year of their collaboration (1930-31), appears to contain compositional or morphological references to almost all the sculptures the two men worked on together. As the most successful three-dimensional sculpture González had made to date, in a sense it represents the culmination of his formation as a sculptor and the point of departure of his mature oeuvre.

González apparently asked Picasso for "permission to work in the same manner as himself, an idea which Picasso naturally encouraged."[36] The meaning of González's request, as we might now perceive, relates quite specifically to motifs and methods on which they had worked together. It refers to the discovery of scrap metal as an acceptable, even desirable, medium that of itself determines images; to the infinite potential of the assemblage principle; and to the translation of conventional subject matter into expressive ciphers or signs.

After 1931 Picasso would embark on a phase of modeled figurative sculpture in the round, whereas González would continue to explore the welded-metal idiom. The years 1932-39 are the most productive of González's career, during which his vision and technique evolved independently from Picasso's direct influence. Although he appreciated the beauty of scrap metal in its raw state, he preferred to cut, shape and polish it according to his own designs. And although he understood the analytical and assemblage processes, he applied them to his own ends, that is, to the improvisation of abstract ideograms.

There are relatively few detailed preparatory sketches for González's sculptures of his mature period. On the contrary, many of the most elaborate drawings were executed after the sculptures, evidence that the imagery was generated by the actual constructive process of assembling his components in space. De-

35. Withers, *Gonzalez,* pp. 42-43, repr.

36. Spies, *Sculpture by Picasso,* p. 73.

37. Interview with Susi Magnelli, the artist's widow, Meudon, April 7, 1982.

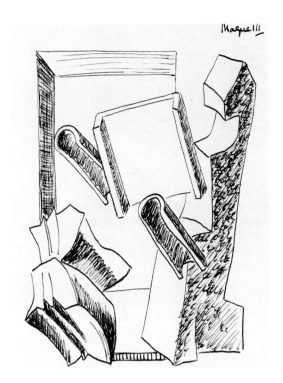

fig. 14
Alberto Magnelli
Sketch for Stones. 1931-33
Ink on paper, 8¼ x 6⅛″ (21 x 15.5 cm.)
Collection Susi Magnelli

fig. 15
Magnelli
Stones. 1934
Gouache on paper, 12⅝ x 9½″ (32 x 24 cm.)
Collection Susi Magnelli

spite the artist's claims that his vision was always based on real observation, his sculptures are less realistic than most Cubist painting. Although a reference to subject matter is indeed present, it is dominated by an abstract architecture or formal language. And just as Cubism is defined by the tension between these two contradictory components, so is González's art defined.

As indicated, González did not hesitate to look toward other artists for a primary formulation of motifs. Yet, transformed, decontextualized and integrated into his own constructive process, this basic vocabulary was of secondary importance. The artist's contacts with Gargallo may have helped him extend his early planar idiom. His work with Picasso helped generate the linear syntax of his middle years. Another encounter, in 1934, would contribute to his transition to a more volumetric style.

In approximately 1934 González met Alberto Magnelli (1888-1971), a Florentine painter living in Paris. The two men may have met through a mutual friend, either Christian Zervos or the artist Luis Fernández. Since 1931 Magnelli had been working on a series of Shattered Stones (*Pierres éclatées*) (see figs. 14, 15) and in 1934 he exhibited thirty paintings and gouaches devoted to this theme at the Galerie Pierre Loeb in Paris. He would develop the series until 1936.

In 1934 or 1935 González apparently visited Magnelli's studio at the Villa Seurat and exclaimed before a painting from this series: "I would like to make a sculpture like that painting."[37] Indeed, without this reference it is difficult to comprehend the blocklike configurations in González's *Seated Woman I* and *II*, executed in 1935 and 1936 (cat. nos. 170, 174), as there is no precedent for them in his work. Of course, true to his temperament and practice, González converted Magnelli's original forms into organic anthropomorphic motifs, adapting the basic configurations to his vision and medium. Full silhouettes and hollow metal volumes soldered so they form squared, pinched or acute angles character-ize this late phase; they are seen in *Woman Combing Her Hair* and *Reclining Figure*, both of ca. 1936 (cat. nos. 193, 188), in *Monsieur Cactus* and *Madame Cactus* (cat. nos. 226, 233), as well as in a whole body of drawings and collages relating to these works. Again a fortuitous encounter catalyzed the development of González's sculptural vision and language.

In any critical study of an artistic phenome-non, the question of influences is central to the determination of originality. They may be as general as those of a period style or the socio-logical, philosophical or political implications of the period in which an artist lived. They may be as specific as the influences on form or process from another artist. Originality, on the other hand, may be defined in terms of form, function, content, materials, or the re-lationship between any or all of these things. Ideally, where the individual makes a lasting contribution to the development of perceptual experience and understanding, one expects him to transcend his influences in order to arrive at his particular expression of genius. Consider, for example, artists of the stature of Picasso or Matisse. The art of their early years manifests a dialectic of exchanges that will subsequently be assimilated and synthe-sized in a personal language of form.

During the abrupt and brief flowering of González's art, the agents of his development are proportionately more visible than those that appear and disappear during a long and sustained career. Apparently this was not an issue for González. He presumably knew that his originality lay elsewhere. Undeniably his contacts with artists and borrowed or recog-nizable morphological components nourished his idiom and provoked permutations within his personal style. But the synthesis he ob-tained, based on a unique understanding of his medium's potential, was his alone. It was this that would earn him the reverence of subsequent generations of sculptors.

A comparison of González's and Picasso's sculptures of this period may help to clarify González's personal contribution. As we have suggested, the fact that Picasso's metal sculp-tures of this period were the translation of a painter's vision distinguishes them basically from González's works. The regular or ir-regular linearity of Picasso's work in three dimensions translated the graphic expressive-ness of his two-dimensional work. The planar motifs also derived directly from the flat sil-houettes or diagrammatically schematized volumes in his paintings. It follows that sculp-tures such as the small *Head* or the *Woman in the Garden* are essentially frontal images. As we move around them, there is no shock of transformation or discovery. In fact, from certain angles of vision the image is impov-erished. Other examples such as the wire constructions, through their symmetry and transparency, may be perceived at a single glance, once again denying the experience in time of progressive revelation that is peculiar to sculpture.

González, on the other hand, grew to recog-nize the difference between a pictorially suc-cessful image and one that is meaningful as sculpture, not only in terms of its three-dimensional specificity, but in terms of the relationship between the image and materials, technique and space. He would discover that an imagery conceived originally in another medium did not necessarily translate as an effective sculpture. He would further con-clude that a perfect or invisible technique ran the risk of denying the definition of sculpture as he came to understand it: in which the qualifications of the materials should be em-phasized precisely through a strongly visible process and a sometimes even crude tech-nique. These would be the carriers of expres-sion and the determinants of form.

One of González's more ambitious early sculptures, *Woman Combing Her Hair* of ca. 1931 (cat. no. 120), reveals the closest par-allel to Picasso's process as a painter. As such, it is perhaps one of González's less mature works, judged according to his later explicit definition of sculpture. Exceptionally, the artist made a complete sequence of studies showing the progressive distillation from an observed reality to a spatially conceived idea. Through an elaborate process he reduced his original theme to its expressive essence, a composition of lines that combines vestiges of outer contours with inner skeletal axes. The resulting sculpture, a truly singular, personal image, is, like the artist's earlier work, most successful from a frontal view.

Yet, at the same time, this piece offers a vivid illustration of the difference between González's and Picasso's sculptures. In comparing González's *Woman Combing Her Hair* with Picasso's *Woman in the Garden*, we realize that we react initially to Picasso's sculpture as a subject, a legible image, and only later does our focus shift to his material and formal invention. By contrast, González's sculpture always solicits us first as an abstract structure—in this instance a kind of angular arabesque—which only with time can be read as an anthropomorphic figure.

A comparison of certain details confirms and clarifies this response. For example, Picasso's linear components, although disjunctive, are nonetheless perceived first as the expressive—and what we have learned to read as idiosyncratic—lines of a pictorial image. However, González's linear components are perceived immediately for what they are: highly irregular, disparate metal lengths and sections, originally designed for other functions. González's sculptures rarely metamorphose as do Picasso's into the subject represented. They remain first and always a construction in metal.

After this period González would not make sequential drawings, as they no longer satisfied his needs. For him, the notion of "drawing in space" referred to the direct process of working in metal. Thus, once he found his personal style, he could not make precise preparatory drawings, because each sculpture's syntax was formulated in the act of making. His was an additive process involving disparate materials (no less disparate for the fact that he shaped many himself) and invoking multiple views. Consequently, he could not *see* a sculpture until it was formed.

For a few major sculptures—*Woman Combing Her Hair* of 1934, *Seated Woman I* and *II*, *Monsieur Cactus* and *Madame Cactus* (cat. nos. 149, 170, 174, 226, 233)—he might explore variations on a theme in sketches in order to find the most expressive postures or relationships among components. But many of these drawings were visual exercises having little to do with the sculptures that followed, because from this time González was thinking in terms of the expressive constructed equivalent of an idea. As he stated himself in about 1930: "A painter or sculptor can give a form to something which has no concrete form: such as light, color, an idea. These forms will of courses be imagined in reference to the human image. Difficult problems to be solved posed by these reinvented planes creating a new architecture."[38]

González's initial evolution from a planar to a linear idiom paradoxically corresponded to an aspiration to arrive at the ultimate expression of sculpture. According to his thinking, only a unified linear figure can be effective as a symbolic form from all sides; a closed mass or volume cannot, because certain angles or surfaces of the sculpture are hidden from the viewer. Thus, he concluded, a linear idiom is the ideal solution for the sculptor.[39]

It must be said finally that Gonzalez's point of departure and his objectives were totally different from those of the artists who inspired him. Picasso's sculptures impress us through their conceptual intelligence and formal inventiveness. González's sculptures move us in other ways. They are compelling because, by virtue of their visible process and technique (and thus the immanent presence of a human hand), they incarnate a precariousness of gesture and emotion. In the linear pieces of approximately 1934 the relationships between the different lengths and sections of metal wire or strips are irregular, nondescriptive and unexpected; yet somehow they express a

38. Unpublished notes, ca. 1930-31. González Estate Archive, Paris.
39. Ibid.

gravity, a tension and an equilibrium that we identify with the postures of the human figure.

Despite the artist's claims that he captured observed reality, González's source of inspiration was an abstraction: not so much the appearance of a human silhouette, but the inner and outer expressive tensions conveyed through its rhythmic articulations. His medium was iron, which contained its own expressive potential. And his destiny was to attempt to unite the two through a "marriage of materials and space."

The real problem to be solved here is not only to strive to make a harmonious work, a fine and perfectly balanced whole—No! But to obtain this [result] through the marriage of materials and space, through the union of real forms with imagined forms, obtained or suggested by established points, or perforations, and, according to the natural law of love, to mingle and make them inseparable one from another, as are the body *and the* spirit. . . .

If the synthetic distortions of materials, color, and light, the perforations, the absence of material planes give the work a mysterious, diabolical and fantastic appearance, then the artist, in addition to idealizing a material which he endows with life, also works with space which will make it sacred.[40]

The "peasant character" of Brancusi should be . . . understood as a state of mind, a particular way of approaching the values of life and art, an aptitude to live a simplified existence, closely attached to elementary realities and in profound communion with nature. . . .[41]

These lines, although referring to Brancusi, could pertain as well to Julio González. Although their origins were not intrinsically comparable (Brancusi was of Rumanian peasant stock, González from a family of Barcelona metalsmiths), the two men shared a state of mind and an existential attitude. They were morally pure, spiritually intense, sober in their life-styles and uncompromising in their ambitions. They also held similar priorities in their art: an almost primitive respect for materials and for manual craft disciplines, a professed devotion to nature and a concerted search for the essence of form and expression. Not surprisingly, they were friends.

Together, yet separately, Brancusi and González transformed the face of twentieth-century sculpture from an art of representational images to an art of invention: an art of formally self-referential objects evoking ideas. A subject was no longer a model to be imitated but a theme on which to compose autonomous formal variations. A material was no longer a medium in the literal sense but the basic determinant of form. A technique was no longer relegated to the hands of a master craftsman or technician but remained in the hands of the artist alone. In fact, it was through the artist's direct realization of his work—Brancusi through direct carving in wood or stone, González through the direct forging of metals—that the new vision of sculpture as we know it today was born.

40. Withers, *Gonzalez,* p. 141, English transl., pp. 134-135.

41. Petru Comarnesco, "Confluences dans la création de Brancusi," in *Témoignages sur Brancusi,* Paris, 1967, p. 21.

NOTES TO THE CATALOGUE

The titles of the following works have been taken from the most comprehensive publications on the artist to date (see below). English translations are by the author. Any parts of the English titles that are absent from the French are additions by the author. Generic or purely descriptive titles (such as those in the Jewelry and Decorative Objects section) have not been given in the French.

All works that were not dated by the artist have been dated by the author, in most cases in collaboration with Jörn Merkert, Berlin, author of the forthcoming catalogue raisonné of González's sculptures, *Werkkatalog der Skulpturen* (see Bibliography, p. 215). These approximate dates are preceded by the notation "ca."

Because González left few titles for his works and dated only his drawings with any constancy, most of the existing titles and dates were originally given by his daughter after his death. Some of these appear somewhat arbitrary, not to say incongruous, in relation to the artist's sensibility. However, for consistency's sake, we have chosen for the most part to respect the given titles, if not the given dates.

Dimensions are given in inches and centimeters, and exclude base or support, unless otherwise noted. Height precedes width precedes depth (when available).

Complete provenance information, bibliographical references for the sculptures, as well as information on the bronze editions will be found in Jörn Merkert's catalogue raisonné.

ABBREVIATIONS:

Barcelona:
Rosa Marie Subirana and Eloisa Sendra, *Donación González*, Barcelona, Museo de Arte Moderno, 1974.

Gibert:
Josette Gibert, *Julio Gonzalez: dessins*, Paris, 1975, vol. I, *Paysages*; vol. II, *Scènes paysannes*; vol. III, *Les Maternités*; vol. IV, *Nus*; vol. V, *Femmes à leur toilette*; vol. VI, *Vie quotidienne*; vol. VII, *Portraits*; vol. VIII, *Projets pour sculptures: Figures*; vol. IX, *Projets pour sculptures: Personnages*.

Madrid:
Guia Catalogo del Museo Español de Arte Contemporáneo de Madrid, ed. Carlos Avean, Madrid, 1975.

Maeght:
Donation González, Saint-Paul-de-Vence, France, 1972.

Tate:
Ronald Alley, *Catalogue of the Tate Gallery's Collection of Modern Art other than works by British Artists*, London, 1981.

Withers:
Josephine Withers, *Julio Gonzalez: Sculpture in Iron*, New York, 1978.

*Indicates not in exhibition.

Studio, Arcueil, 1937

I. PORTRAITS AND SELF-PORTRAITS

1
Pablo Picasso
Portrait of Julio González. 1902
(Portrait de Julio González)
Watercolor and ink on paper, 11½ x 9½"
(29 x 24 cm.)
Signed and inscribed l.l.: *Recuerdo para Julio
Gonzales/de su amigo Picasso*
Courtesy David Grob, London

REFERENCE:
Christian Zervos, *Pablo Picasso*, Paris, 1969,
vol. 21, p. 74, no. 189

2
Self-Portrait. ca. 1914-17
(Autoportrait)
Charcoal and pastel on red-brown paper, 12⅞ x 9⅞"
(32.6 x 25 cm.)
Not signed or dated
Collection Museo de Arte Moderno, Barcelona, Gift
of Roberta González, 1972

REFERENCES:
Barcelona, p. 22, no. 73, pl. 7 (MAB 113.452)
Gibert, vol. VII, p. 53, repr.

3
Self-Portrait. 1938
(Autoportrait)
Pencil on paper, 7⅜ x 4¼″ (19.5 x 10.8 cm.)
Dated l.r.: *14-5-38.* Not signed
Collection Carmen Martinez and Viviane
Grimminger, Paris

4
Self-Portrait. ca. 1942
(Autoportrait)
Oil on cardboard, 7⅛ x 5½″ (18 x 14 cm.)
Not signed or dated
Private Collection

II. PAINTINGS

González's initial ambition was to be a painter. Yet
for the most part his paintings, executed in a flat
fresco style, were unremarkable. The earliest paintings and comparable drawings show the influence of
Degas (in their dry or luminous pastel color), early
Picasso (in the sentimental interpretation of female
subject matter), and Puvis de Chavannes who was
widely admired in Paris and Barcelona around the
turn of the century (in their flat color, Classical feeling and monumental scale). Some paintings initiate
themes that González would subsequently elaborate
in his sculpture, in particular the Woman and Child
and the Woman Fixing (or Combing) Her Hair
motifs (cat. nos. 8, 7). The dates given here are
based on stylistic considerations.

6
Large Nude. ca. 1908-10
(Grand nu)
Oil on canvas, 68½ x 26⅝″ (174 x 67.5 cm.)
Not signed or dated
Collection Musée National d'Art Moderne, Centre
Georges Pompidou, Paris, Don de Mme R. Gonzalez

7
Woman Fixing a Young Girl's Hair. ca. 1908-10
(Femme coiffant une jeune fille)
Oil on canvas, 48⅞ x 31⅛″ (123 x 79 cm.)
Not signed or dated
Collection Museo Español de Arte Contemporáneo,
Madrid (Donación Roberta González)
REFERENCE:
Madrid, p. 90 (P. 1171)

8
Mother and Child. ca. 1914-18
(Maternité)
Oil and charcoal on cardboard, 30 x 20⅞"
(76.2 x 53 cm.)
Not signed or dated
Collection Carmen Martinez and Viviane
Grimminger, Paris

III. JEWELRY AND DECORATIVE OBJECTS

Throughout his lifetime, González worked as a decorative metalsmith. Starting before 1900 in the family metalworking shop in Barcelona, where he worked alongside his father Concordio and his brother Joan, he would pursue this occupation as a source of income until his final years. The following pieces illustrate his adeptness at working raw nonprecious metals and plying them to ornamental ends.

None of these items can be dated with complete precision, because González tended to conform to conservative decorative conventions; for the same reason, the works show little stylistic evolution. Nonetheless, some examples (cat. nos. 12, 13) refer closely to the Barcelona turn-of-the-century *modernista* style; whereas *Small Baroque Mask* and *Japanese Mask* (cat. nos. 31, 32), traditionally dated 1927-28 and 1928 (despite a hammered fabrication identical to that seen in *Tray with Daisy Motif* dated ca. 1918-25 [cat. no. 30]), reflect an ambition to create more autonomous, less functional objects. All other pieces have been dated on the basis of sophistication of concept or execution, or indications found in family records or given by the owners.

9
Bouquet of Flowers. ca. 1890-1900
Copper and iron, 25⅝ x 9⅞ x 5⅞" (65 x 25 x 15 cm.)
Not signed or dated
Collection Museo de Arte Moderno, Barcelona, Gift of Roberta González, 1972

REFERENCE:
Barcelona, p. 33, no. 200 (MAB 113.596)

This piece was made in González's father's metalworking studio in Barcelona. Whether it was made by Julio, his older brother Joan, or the two brothers working together has never been established.

10
Inkwell with Butterfly Motif. ca. 1890-1900
Iron, 3⅜ x 3½ x 5½" (8.5 x 9 x 14 cm.)
Not signed or dated
Collection Museo de Arte Moderno, Barcelona, Gift
of Roberta González, 1972
REFERENCE:
Barcelona, p. 33, no. 202 (MAB 113.598)

11a
Pendant. ca. 1900-10
Gold with crystal bead, 2 x 1⅜" (5 x 3.3 cm.)
Not signed or dated
Collection Carmen Martinez and Viviane
Grimminger, Paris

11b
Pendant. ca. 1900-10
Gilded copper with rose crystal bead and pearl,
1⅞ x 1⅝" (4.5 x 4 cm.)
Not signed or dated
Collection Carmen Martinez and Viviane
Grimminger, Paris

12
Pendant. ca. 1900-10
Iron, 2⅜ x 2⅜ x ⅝" (5.9 x 5.9 x 1.5 cm.)
Not signed or dated
Collection Museo de Arte Moderno, Barcelona, Gift
of Roberta González, 1972
REFERENCE:
Barcelona, p. 33, no. 196 (MAB 113.591)

13
Buckle. ca. 1900-10
Iron, 6⅝ x 4½" (11.5 x 6.5 cm.)
Not signed or dated
Private Collection

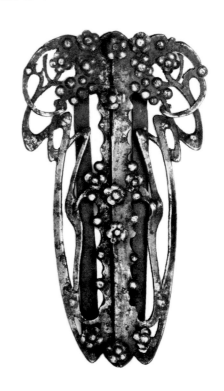

14a
Set of Four Buttons. ca. 1900-10
Silver with turquoise and ruby chips, each ⅞″
(2.1 cm.) diameter
Not signed or dated
Private Collection

14b
Set of Five Buttons. ca. 1900-10
Hammered silver, each ⅜″ (1 cm.) diameter
Not signed or dated
Private Collection

15
Necklace. ca. 1910-20
Copper with green beads, 19⅜″ (49.2 cm.) open
length
Not signed or dated
Collection Carmen Martinez and Viviane
Grimminger, Paris

16
Necklace with Fuchsia Motif. ca. 1916-25
Silver with amethyst, 18⅛″ (46 cm.) open length
Stamped on reverse of pendant with monogram: *G*
Collection Musée National d'Art Moderne, Centre
Georges Pompidou, Paris, Don de M. T. Roux

17
Necklace. ca. 1916-25
Silver-plated metal with green cornalines, 16½″
(42 cm.) open length
Not signed or dated
Collection Museo de Arte Moderno, Barcelona, Gift
of Roberta González, 1972
REFERENCE:
Barcelona, p. 33, no. 195, pl. 12 (MAB 113.587)

18
Ring with Acorn Motif. ca. 1914-25
Gilded iron with calcedonia, 1 x ⅞ x ¾″
(2.5 x 2.2 x 1.9 cm.)
Not signed or dated
Collection Museo de Arte Moderno, Barcelona, Gift
of Roberta González, 1972
REFERENCE:
Barcelona, p. 33, no. 193 (MAB 113.590)

19
Ring. ca. 1914-25
Silver with turquoise, 1¼ x 1 x ¾″ (3 x 2.5 x 2 cm.)
Stamped with monogram: *G*
Collection Museo de Arte Moderno, Barcelona, Gift
of Roberta González, 1972
REFERENCE:
Barcelona, p. 33, no. 192 (MAB 113.589)

20
Ring. ca. 1914-25
Silver with red stone, 1¼″ (3 cm.) high
Stamped with monogram: *G*
Collection Musée National d'Art Moderne, Centre
Georges Pompidou, Paris, Don de Mme R. Gonzalez

21
Ring with Dragon Motif. ca. 1914-25
Forged iron with uncut topaz, 1¼″ (3 cm.) high
Not signed or dated
Collection Musée National d'Art Moderne, Centre
Georges Pompidou, Paris, Don de M. T. Roux

22
Ring. ca. 1914-25
Silver with rubies and opal, 1⅛ x 1¼ x 1″
(2.9 x 3 x 2.5 cm.)
Not signed or dated
Collection Viviane Grimminger, Paris

23
Ring with Fleur-de-Lis Motif. ca. 1929
Iron and silver with synthetic sapphire, ½″ (1.7 cm.)
high
Not signed or dated
Collection Louise Varèse, New York

 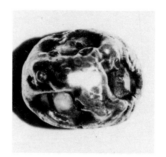

24
Cup and Saucer. ca. 1915-25
Hammered and etched silver, cup 2 x 2⅝"
(5 x 6.5 cm.); saucer 5⅜" (13.2 cm.) diameter
Not signed or dated
Collection Museo de Arte Moderno, Barcelona, Gift
of Roberta González, 1972
REFERENCE:
Barcelona, p. 33, no. 199 (MAB 113.595)

25
Letter Opener with Grasshopper Motif. ca. 1915-25
Silver and gold, 9⅛ x 1" (23 x 2.5 cm.)
Not signed or dated
Collection Musée National d'Art Moderne, Centre
Georges Pompidou, Paris, Don de Mme R. Gonzalez

26
Hand Mirror. ca. 1915-25
Mirror with cast pewter handle, 15¾ x 5½ x ¾"
(40 x 14 x 2 cm.)
Not signed or dated
Collection Museo Español de Arte Contemporáneo,
Madrid (Donación Roberta González)
REFERENCE:
Madrid, p. 220 (AD-1)

27
Bracelet. ca. 1925-30
Copper and iron, 2¾ x 2⅜ x ⅜″ (7 x 6 x .6 cm.)
Not signed or dated
Collection Museo Español de Arte Contemporáneo,
Madrid (Donación Roberta González)
REFERENCE:
Madrid, p. 219 (AD-6)

28
Decorative Motif. ca. 1925-35
Hammered nickle-silver with blue cornaline, 2½″
(6.3 cm.) diameter
Not signed or dated
Collection Carmen Martinez and Viviane
Grimminger, Paris

29
Necklace. ca. 1930-40
Silver, 16¼″ (41.2 cm.) open length
Not signed or dated
Collection Carmen Martinez and Viviane
Grimminger, Paris

30
Tray with Daisy Motif. ca. 1918-25
Etched copper and iron, 7⅞ x 7½″ (20 x 19 cm.)
Not signed or dated
Collection Museo Español de Arte Contemporáneo,
Madrid (Donación Roberta González)
REFERENCE:
Madrid, p. 220 (AD-14)

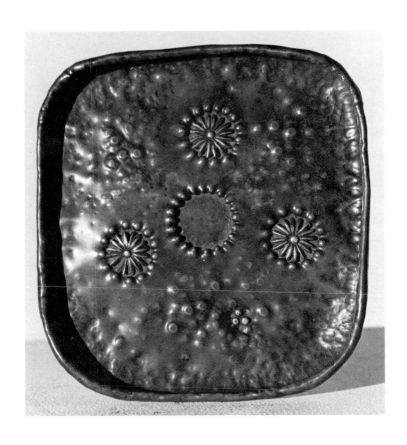

31
Small Baroque Mask. ca. 1927-28
(Petit masque baroque)
Iron, 4⅞ x 4¼ x ⅞″ (12.5 x 10.8 x 2 cm.)
Not signed or dated
Collection Carmen Martinez and Viviane
Grimminger, Paris
REFERENCE:
Withers, p. 31, fig. 13, p. 156, no. 5

32
Japanese Mask (Portrait of Foujita). ca. 1928
(Masque japonais)
Forged bronze, 7⅛″ (18 cm.) high
Not signed or dated
The Arthur and Madeleine Lejwa Collection,
New York
REFERENCE:
Withers, p. 45, fig. 24, pp. 157-158, no. 22

33
Crucifix. ca. 1939-41
Hammered silver, 1¼ x 1⅛″ (3.1 x 2.8 cm.)
Not signed or dated
Collection Carmen Martinez and Viviane
Grimminger, Paris

34
Crucifix. ca. 1939-41
Hammered silver, 2 x 1¾″ (5 x 4.3 cm.)
Not signed or dated
Collection Museo de Arte Moderno, Barcelona, Gift
of Roberta González, 1972

REFERENCE:
Barcelona, p. 33, no. 197 (MAB 113.593)

35
Crucifix. ca. 1942
Iron, 2⅛ x 1¼ x ¼″ (5.5 x 3.2 x .5 cm.)
Not signed or dated
Collection Museo Español de Arte Contemporáneo,
Madrid (Donación Roberta González)

REFERENCE:
Madrid, p. 220 (AD-3)

IV. DRAWINGS AND SCULPTURE

González drew prolifically all his life. His earliest drawings (those executed prior to ca. 1914) are characteristic of the turn-of-the-century School of Barcelona style in their sentimental subject matter and fluid technique, even though he had been living in Paris since 1900. During the initial phases of González's activity as a sculptor, he made many preliminary drawings as he searched to translate a motif into a sculptural solution. Many times he cut out these drawings in the same way he would cut the metal plates for the flat frontal pieces of 1929-30 (see for example cat. nos. 72b, 81a, b, 90a, b).

Starting in 1932, after mastering the process of improvising with metal in space, he executed fewer truly preparatory sketches directly related to specific sculptures. Although González may have explored in drawings variations on a theme he considered particularly significant, the sculpture itself would often be quite different. Sometimes he made elaborate drawings after the sculpture was finished.

Late in the artist's lifetime, during the wartime period when he did not have a metalworking studio, he produced many drawings in both abstract and naturalistic styles that, like this earliest drawings, seem to have been ends in themselves. These works manifest an explicit anxiety that is present, though in a latent state, throughout his oeuvre and cannot be dismissed as relating only to the Spanish Civil War and World War II (which nonetheless affected him deeply). It is furthermore interesting to note Picasso's influence emerging strongly once again in the artist's late graphic work (see cat. nos. 216, 227, 245). Clearly Picasso was a conscious or subconscious model for González throughout his life.

González dated few of his sculptures himself. Many of the sculptures in the following sequence have been redated, based on documents in the González Estate Archive, exhibition histories, a relationship to drawings, and plausible stylistic groupings. A few of the sculptures have been renamed, once again based on documentary evidence (cat. nos. 226, 233) or stylistic analysis (cat. nos. 101, 102).[1]

In general, the works seem to follow a progression from a planar idiom, to a linear "drawing in space" and finally to a more volumetric style. At intervals during the artist's career, he executed works in a more naturalistic mode that seem to reflect a nostalgia for a more legible, concrete form of expression. This is particularly true of his final years, during which his deep concern for world events motivated attempts to make more socially effective (because more universally comprehensible) symbolic figurative sculptures.

[1]. New dates and titles have been discussed at length with Jörn Merkert. In the present publication, a new title appears first, followed by the traditional one in parentheses.

36a
Young Woman Combing Her Hair. 1904
(Jeune femme se coiffant)
Purple ink and wash on paper, irregular, ca. 8 x 4⅞″ (20.3 x 12.3 cm.)
Signed and dated l.l.: *juli / 10 / 904*
Collection Carmen Martinez and Viviane Grimminger, Paris

36b
Long Hair. 1904
(Longs cheveux)
Pencil and brown wash on paper mounted on green paper, 7⅛ x 3½″ (18.1 x 9 cm.)
Signed and dated l.r.: *juli / 10 / 904*
Collection Carmen Martinez and Viviane Grimminger, Paris

36c
Long Hair. 1904
(La Longue chevelure)
India ink and wash on paper, 7⅛ x 4½″ (18 x 11.5 cm.)
Signed and dated l.r.: *juli / 10 / 904*
Collection Carmen Martinez and Viviane Grimminger, Paris

36d
Two Women Combing Their Hair. 1904
(Deux femmes se coiffant)
Pencil and watercolor on paper, 8 x 6⅛″ (20.2 x 15.7 cm.)
Signed and dated l.l.: *juli / 10 / 904*
Collection Carmen Martinez and Viviane Grimminger, Paris

REFERENCES:
Gibert, vol. V, pp. 7, 6, 8, 10, reprs.

37
Mother and Child. 1906
(Maternité)
Brown ink and wash on cream paper, 12¼ x 7⅞"
(31 x 19.9 cm.)
Signed and dated l.r.: *juli / 1 / 906*
Collection Museo de Arte Moderno, Barcelona, Gift
of Roberta González, 1972
REFERENCES:
Barcelona, p. 20, no. 50 (MAB 113.522)
Gibert, vol. III, p. 16, repr.

38
Mother and Child. 1906
(Maternité)
Ink and brown wash on ivory tracing paper, 10 x 5⅝"
(25.3 x 14.4 cm.)
Signed and dated: l.r.: *juli / 2 / 906*
Courtesy The Pace Gallery, New York
REFERENCE:
Gibert, vol. III, p. 21, repr.

39
Caped Mother and Child. ca. 1910-14
(Maternité au capuchon)
Terra-cotta, 8⅝ x 2½ x 3¼″ (22 x 6.5 x 8.3 cm.)
Signed on back of base: *Gonzalez* Not dated
Collection Carmen Martinez and Viviane
Grimminger, Paris

40
Sulky Profile. ca. 1907-09
(Profil boudeur)
Pastel on paper, 12⅞ x 9⅜" (31.5 x 23.9 cm.)
Not signed or dated
Collection Carmen Martinez and Viviane
Grimminger, Paris
REFERENCE:
Gibert, vol. VII, p. 10, repr.

41
Woman Knitting. ca. 1907-09
(Femme travaillant)
Pencil and watercolor on blue-gray paper, 9⅞ x 6⅜"
(25 x 16.3 cm.)
Not signed or dated
Collection Carmen Martinez and Viviane
Grimminger, Paris
REFERENCE:
Gibert, vol. VI, p. 15, repr.

42
Seated Woman with Corset. ca. 1909
(Femme au corset assise)
Charcoal on paper, 14¾ x 10⅞″ (37.5 x 27.7 cm.)
Not signed or dated
Collection Museo de Arte Moderno, Barcelona, Gift
of Roberta González, 1972

REFERENCES:
Barcelona, p. 20, no. 53 (MAB 113.500)
Gibert, vol. V, p. 110, repr.

43
Young Woman in an Armchair. ca. 1909-10
(Jeune femme dans un fauteuil)
Charcoal and pastel on paper, 11⅛ x 8⅞″
(28.2 x 22.6 cm.)
Not signed or dated
Collection Carmen Martinez and Viviane
Grimminger, Paris

REFERENCE:
Gibert, vol. V, p. 22, repr.

44

Portrait of Jeanne. 1910
(Portrait de Jeanne)
Pencil on paper, 13 x 11⅜″ (33.1 x 28.9 cm.)
Signed and dated l.r.: *J. L. Gonzalez / 910*
Collection Carmen Martinez and Viviane
Grimminger, Paris

REFERENCE:
Gibert, vol. VII, p. 33, repr.

45

Woman Ironing. ca. 1910-14
(La Repasseuse)
Charcoal on paper, 9⅞ x 6¼″ (25 x 16 cm.)
Not signed or dated
Collection Carmen Martinez and Viviane
Grimminger, Paris

REFERENCE:
Gibert, vol. VI, p. 19, repr.

46
Woman Bathing Herself. ca. 1910-14
(Femme penchée se lavant)
Charcoal and pastel on paper, 17⅜ x 12⅝″
(44 x 32 cm.)
Not signed or dated
Collection Moderna Museet, Stockholm

REFERENCE:
Gibert, vol. IV, p. 18, repr.

47
Nude in Profile with Chair. ca. 1910-14
(Nu de profil à la chaise)
Charcoal and pastel on paper, 12⅞ x 9⅞″
(32.7 x 25.2 cm.)
Signed l.r.: *juli* Not dated
Collection Museo de Arte Moderno, Barcelona, Gift
of Roberta González, 1972

REFERENCES:
Barcelona, p. 21, no. 62
Gibert, vol. IV, p. 23, repr.

48

Portrait of a Proud Young Woman. ca. 1910-14
(Portrait de jeune femme fière)
Charcoal and pastel on cream paper, 18⅝ x 12¼″
(47.4 x 31.2 cm.)
Not signed or dated
Collection Museo de Arte Moderno, Barcelona, Gift
of Roberta González, 1972

REFERENCES:
Barcelona, p. 21, no. 59
Gibert, vol. VII, p. 26, repr.

49
Face of a Young Woman. ca. 1914
(Visage de jeune femme)
Pencil and pastel on red paper, 12⅝ x 9⅞″
(32 x 25 cm.)
Not signed or dated
Collection Museo Español de Arte Contemporáneo,
Madrid (Donación Roberta González)

REFERENCES:
Madrid, p. 171 (D-379)
Gibert, vol. VII, p. 24, repr.

50
Pilar and Lola. ca. 1914-18
(Pilar et Lola)
Pencil and pastel on red paper, 6¼ x 9⅞″
(16.5 x 25 cm.)
Not signed or dated
Collection Museo Español de Arte Contemporáneo,
Madrid (Donación Roberta González)

REFERENCES:
Madrid, p. 171 (D-377)
Gibert, vol. VII, p. 21, repr.

51
Portrait of Pilar. 1913
(Portrait de Pilar)
Hammered copper, 12 x 8¼ x 5⅜″
(30.5 x 21 x 13.5 cm.)
Signed and dated l.l.: *Gonzalez / 1913*
Collection Musée National d'Art Moderne, Centre
Georges Pompidou, Paris, Don de Mme R. Gonzalez

52
Portrait of Alberta. 1913
(Portrait d'Alberta)
Hammered copper, 11⅞ x 8⅜″ (30.2 x 21.2 cm.)
Signed and dated l.l.: *Gonzalez* / *1913*
Collection Museo de Arte Moderno, Barcelona, Gift
of Roberta González, 1972

REFERENCE:
Barcelona, p. 15, no. 3 (MAB 113.438)

53
Head with Curls. 1921
(Tête aux boucles)
Hammered copper, 8⅝ x 7½ x 4″ (22 x 19 x 10 cm.)
Signed and dated on reverse: *j. Gonzalez* / *1921*
Collection Museo de Arte Moderno, Barcelona, Gift
of Roberta González, 1972

REFERENCE:
Barcelona, p. 15, no. 7 (MAB 113.694)

54

Seated Nude from the Back. ca. 1918
(Nu assis de dos)
Pencil and pastel on brown paper, 12¾ x 9⅞″
(32.5 x 25 cm.)
Not signed or dated
Collection Museo Español de Arte Contemporáneo,
Madrid (Donación Roberta González)

REFERENCES:
Madrid, p. 171 (D-383)
Gibert, vol. IV, p. 46, repr.

55
Reclining Nude with Draped Cloth. ca. 1918
(Nu allongé avec draperie)
Pencil and pastel on brown paper, 11⅜ x 15⅜"
(29 x 39 cm.)
Not signed or dated
Collection Museo Español de Arte Contemporáneo,
Madrid (Donación Roberta González)

REFERENCES:
Madrid, p. 171 (D-369)
Gibert, vol. IV, p. 46, repr.

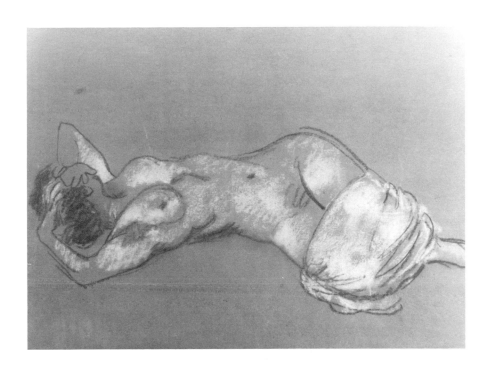

56
Small Bowed Seated Woman. ca. 1914
(Femme assise penchée)
Terra-cotta on plaster base, 6½ x 4¾ x 6⅛″
(16.5 x 12 x 15.5 cm.)
Not signed or dated
Collection Carmen Martinez and Viviane
Grimminger, Paris

57
Reclining Nude. 1914
(Nu allongé)
Terra-cotta, 3¾ x 8½ x 4½″ (9.5 x 21.5 x 11.5 cm.)
Signed and dated on base near left hip:
j. Gonzalez / 1914
Collection Carmen Martinez and Viviane
Grimminger, Paris

58
Couple. ca. 1914
(Le Couple)
Terra-cotta, 5⅜ x 6¾ x 5″ (13.5 x 17 x 12.5 cm.)
Not signed or dated
Collection Carmen Martinez and Viviane
Grimminger, Paris

REFERENCE:
Withers, p. 49, fig. 29

59
Catalan Peasant Woman. ca. 1914-18
(Paysanne catalane)
Pastel on medium brown paper, 12¾ x 9⅝″
(32.4 x 24.5 cm.)
Not signed or dated
Collection Carmen Martinez and Viviane
Grimminger, Paris

REFERENCE:
Gilbert, vol. II, p. 28, repr.

60
Peasant Woman in Blue with Large Basket. 1919
(Paysanne en bleu au grand panier)
Pastel on gray paper, 9⅞ x 12⅞″ (25 x 32.8 cm.)
Signed and dated l.r.: *Gonzalez / 1919*
Collection Museo de Arte Moderno, Barcelona, Gift
of Roberta González, 1972

REFERENCES:
Barcelona, p. 23, no. 80 (MAB 113.492)
Gibert, vol. II, p. 43, repr.

61

Large Trees. 1919
(Les Grands arbres)
Pastel on red-brown paper, 12¾ x 9⅝″
(32.5 x 24.5 cm.)
Signed and dated l.l.: *Gonzalez / 1919*
Collection The Trustees of the Tate Gallery, London

REFERENCES:
Tate, p. 312, repr. (T. 1598)
Gibert, vol. II, p. 36, repr.

62
Portrait of Marie-Thérèse with a Hat. ca. 1926
(Portrait de Marie-Thérèse au chapeau)
Pencil on gray paper, 11⅞ x 7¾″ (30.3 x 19.7 cm.)
Not signed or dated
Private Collection

63
Portrait of Marie-Thérèse. 1927
(Portrait de Marie-Thérèse)
Pencil on paper, 9⅞ x 6¼″ (25 x 16 cm.)
Signed and dated l.r.: *j.G. / 1927*
Private Collection

64

Head with Hat. ca. 1928-29

(Tête au chapeau)

Copper, 4⅞ x 3¾″ (12.5 x 9.5 cm.)

Not signed or dated

Collection Museo de Arte Moderno, Barcelona, Gift
of Roberta González, 1972

REFERENCE:

Barcelona, p. 15, no. 9 (MAB 113.443)

65

Head with Hat. 1929

(Tête au chapeau)

Iron, 5⅞ x 5½″ (15 x 14 cm.)

Signed and dated l.r.: *Gonzalez / 1929*

Collection Museo de Arte Moderno, Barcelona, Gift
of Roberta González, 1972

REFERENCE:

Barcelona, p. 16, no. 13 (MAB 113.690)

66a
Studies for "Face in the Sun." ca. 1929
(Etudes pour "Visage au soleil")
Pencil, India ink and wash on paper, 6⅛ x 4⅜″
(15.7 x 11.1 cm.)
Not signed or dated; inscribed u.l.: *1.2.4.5.6.*
Collection Carmen Martinez and Viviane
Grimminger, Paris

66b
Studies for "Pilar in the Sun." ca. 1929
(Etudes pour "Pilar au soleil")
Pencil, India ink and wash on paper, 9½ x 6⅛″
(24 x 15.7 cm.)
Not signed or dated
Collection Carmen Martinez and Viviane
Grimminger, Paris

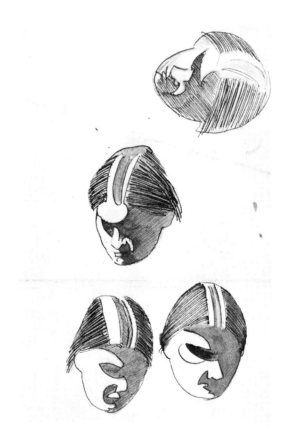

66c

Study for "Aunt Pilar in the Sun." 1929
(Etude pour "Tia Pilar au soleil")
Pencil, brown ink and wash on paper, 6¼ x 6⅜″
(16 x 16.3 cm.)
Signed and dated l.l.: *j.G. / 1929*
Collection Carmen Martinez and Viviane
Grimminger, Paris

REFERENCES:
Gibert, vol. VIII, pp. 12, 13, 10, reprs.

67

Mask of "Roberta in the Sun." ca. 1929
(Masque de "Roberta au soleil")
Iron, 7⅛ x 6½ x 2⅝″ (18 x 16.5 x 6.5 cm.)
Not signed or dated
Collection Carmen Martinez and Viviane
Grimminger, Paris

REFERENCE:
Withers, p. 158, no. 27

68
Mask of "Pilar in the Sun." 1929
(Masque de Pilar "au soleil")
Iron, 7⅛″ (18 cm.) high
Signed and dated l.l.: *G. / 1929*
Collection Musée National d'Art Moderne, Centre
Georges Pompidou, Paris, Don de Mme. R. Gonzalez
REFERENCE:
Withers, p. 49, fig. 31, p. 158, no. 26

69
Studies for "Mask Called 'The Poet.' " ca. 1929
(Quatres petites têtes—Etudes pour "Masque dit
'Le Poète'")
Ink and wash on paper, 4⅞ x 6½" (12.5 x 16.3 cm.)
Not signed or dated
Courtesy Galerie de France, Paris

REFERENCE:
Gibert, vol. VIII, p. 17, repr.

70
Mask Called "The Poet." 1929
(Masque dit "Le Poète")
Iron, 10¼ x 9⅝ x 1⅜" (26 x 24.5 x 3.5 cm.)
Signed and dated l.r.: *Gonzalez* / *1929*
Private Collection

REFERENCE:
Withers, p. 158, no. 25

*71
Seated Woman. 1929
(Femme assise)
Pencil and ink on paper, 4⅜ x 3¾″ (11 x 9.8 cm.)
Signed and dated l.r.: *j.G. / 1929*
Private Collection

72a
Still Life. ca. 1929
(Nature morte)
Pencil and ink on paper, 7⅞ x 6⅛″ (20.1 x 15.5 cm.)
Not signed or dated
Courtesy The Pace Gallery, New York

72b
Still Life. ca. 1929
(Nature morte)
Pencil and India ink on paper mounted on light blue
cardboard, drawing 6⅛ x 3¼″ (15.5 x 9 cm.); mount
9⅞ x 6⅜″ (25 x 16.3 cm.)
Not signed or dated
Collection Carmen Martinez and Viviane
Grimminger, Paris

73
Seated Nude in Profile. 1929
(Nu assis de profil)
Iron, 4⅞ x 5⅝″ (12.5 x 14.3 cm.)
Signed and dated l.r.: *G. / 1929*
Collection Museo de Arte Moderno, Barcelona, Gift
of Roberta González, 1972

REFERENCES:
Barcelona, p. 16, no. 14 (MAB 113.442)
Withers, p. 156, no. 6

74
Still Life II. ca. 1929
(Nature morte II)
Iron, 8¼ x 8¼″ (21 x 21 cm.)
Not signed or dated
Collection Museo de Arte Moderno, Barcelona, Gift
of Roberta González, 1972

REFERENCES:
Barcelona, p. 15, no. 10, pl. 2 (MAB 113.441)
Withers, p. 49, fig. 30, p. 157, no. 21

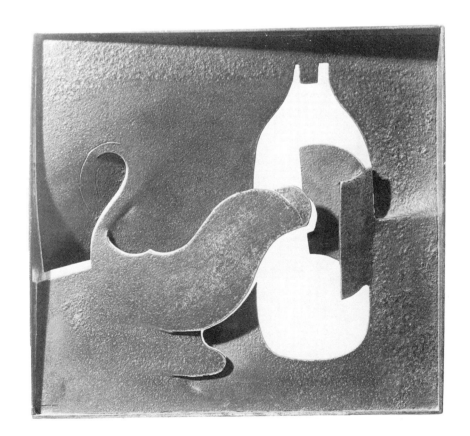

75

Double Mask. 1929
(Double masque)
India ink and wash on paper, 9½ x 12¼″
(24 x 31 cm.)
Signed and dated l.l.: *j. Gonzalez / 1929*; l.r.:
j. Gonzalez / 1929
Collection Museo Español de Arte Contemporáneo,
Madrid (Donación Roberta González)
REFERENCES:
Madrid, p. 172 (D-432)
Gibert, vol. VIII, p. 6, repr.

76

Mask "with Cheekbone." 1929
(Masque "à la pommette")
Forged bronze, 10⅛″ (25.6 cm.) high
Signed and dated l.l.: *j. Gonzalez / 1929*
Private Collection

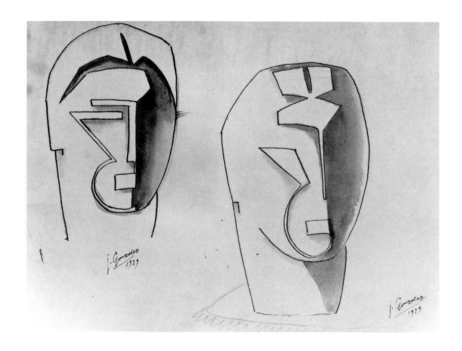

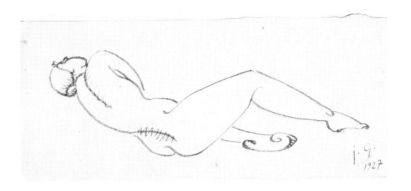

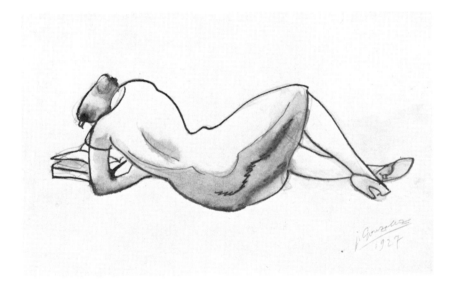

77a
Reclining Nude. 1927
(Nu étendu)
Blue ink on paper, 3¼ x 7½″ (8.2 x 19 cm.)
Signed and dated: l.r.: *j. G.* / *1927*
Collection Carmen Martinez and Viviane
Grimminger, Paris

77b
Reclining Woman Reading. 1927
(Femme couchée lisant)
Pencil, India ink and wash on paper, 6⅝ x 9⅞″
(16.7 x 25 cm.)
Signed and dated l.r.: *j. Gonzalez* / *1927*
Courtesy The Pace Gallery, New York

REFERENCES:
Gibert, vol. IV, p. 84, repr.; vol. VI, p. 40, repr.

78
Reclining Woman Reading. 1930
(Femme allongée lisant)
Forged bronze, 4¾ x 10½″ (12.2 x 26.6 cm.)
Signed and dated l.l.: *j. Gonzalez* / *1930*
Courtesy Galerie de France, Paris

REFERENCE:
Withers, p. 159, no. 35

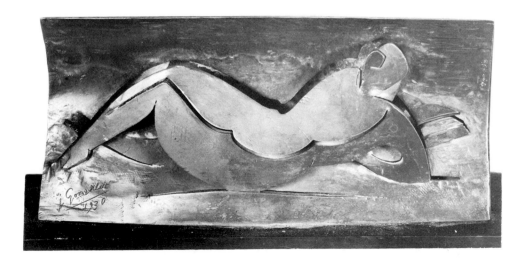

79
Small Don Quixote Mask. 1930
(Petit masque Don Quichotte)
Iron, 4⅞ x 2¾ x 1⅝″ (12.5 x 7 x 4 cm.)
Signed and dated on reverse: *1930 / j. Gonzalez*
Collection Museo de Arte Moderno, Barcelona, Gift
of Roberta González, 1972

REFERENCES:
Barcelona, p. 16, no. 16, pl. 3 (MAB 113.691)
Withers, p. 46, fig. 26, p. 158, no. 30

80
Reclining Head Called "Spanish Mask." 1930
(Tête couchée dite "Masque espagnol")
Forged bronze, 6¾ x 9⅞ x 1½″ (17 x 25 x 4 cm.)
Signed and dated on reverse: *j. Gonzalez / 1930*
Collection Museo Español de Arte Contemporáneo,
Madrid (Donación Roberta González)

REFERENCES:
Madrid, p. 147 (E-473)
Withers, p. 43, fig. 22, pp. 158-159, no. 32

81a
Four Small Cutout Heads. ca. 1930
(Quatre petites têtes découpées)
Pencil and ink on various papers mounted on white
cardboard, mount 4½ x 6⅛″ (11.5 x 15.5 cm.)
Not signed or dated
Collection Carmen Martinez and Viviane
Grimminger, Paris

81b
Study for "Mask 'My.' " ca. 1930
(Etude pour "Masque 'My'")
Pencil on beige cardboard mounted on cardboard,
drawing 1⅝ x 1¼″ (4.1 x 3.2 cm.); mount
4⅜ x 3¼″ (11.1 x 8.2 cm.)
Not signed or dated
Collection Carmen Martinez and Viviane
Grimminger, Paris

82
Mask "My." ca. 1930
(Masque "My")
Iron, 7⅞″ (20 cm.) high
Not signed or dated
Private Collection, Paris
REFERENCE:
Withers, p. 157, no. 14

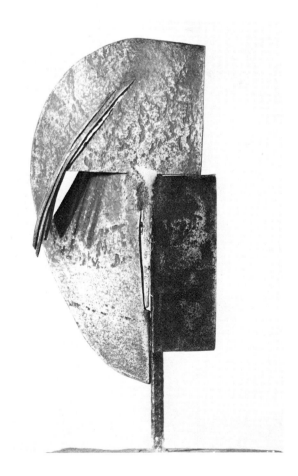

83a
Inscrutable Face. ca. 1930
(Visage fermé)
Pencil, India ink and wash on paper, 6¾ x 4¾″
(17 x 12.2 cm.)
Not signed or dated
Collection Carmen Martinez and Viviane
Grimminger, Paris

83b
Face with Earrings. ca. 1930
(Visage aux boucles d'oreille)
Pencil, India ink and wash on paper, 4¼ x 3¾″
(10.7 x 9.7 cm.)
Not signed or dated
Collection Carmen Martinez and Viviane
Grimminger, Paris

REFERENCES:
Gibert, vol. VIII, pp. 25, 24, reprs.

84
Angular Head. ca. 1930
(Tête aigüe)
Iron, 12¼″ (31 cm.) high
Not signed or dated
Collection K. N. Hoss, Paris

REFERENCE:
Withers, p. 48, fig. 32, p. 159, no. 36

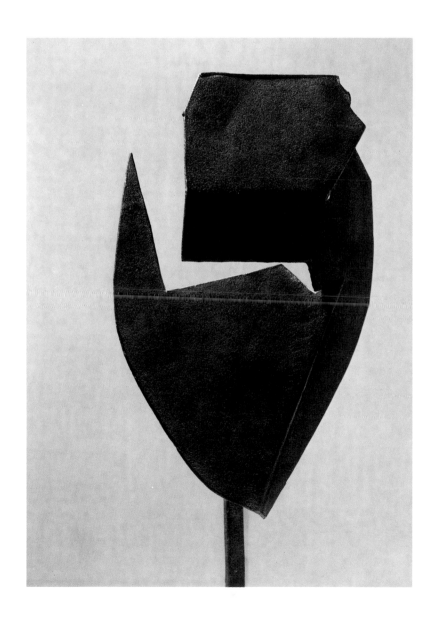

85
Marie-Thérèse with a Scarf. ca. 1926-29
(Marie-Thérèse au fichu)
Pencil on light blue paper mounted on brown paper,
10⅛ x 7″ (25.8 x 17.9 cm.)
Not signed or dated
Collection Carmen Martinez and Viviane
Grimminger, Paris
REFERENCE:
Gibert, vol. VII, p. 86, repr.

86
The Montserrat. ca. 1930
(La Montserrat)
Pencil on paper, 6½ x 4½″ (16.5 x 11.3 cm.)
Not signed or dated; inscribed on base:
LA MONSERRAT [sic]
Collection Hans Hartung, Antibes
REFERENCE:
Gibert, vol. II, p. 243, repr.

87
Head of the Small Montserrat. ca. 1930
(Tête de la petite Montserrat)
Iron, 12¾″ (32.5 cm.) high
Not signed or dated; inscribed on base:
LA MOTSERRAT [sic]
Collection Mrs. Andrew Fuller, New York

REFERENCE:
Withers, p. 47, fig. 27, p. 160, no. 45

88
Reclining Figure. ca. 1929
(Personnage allongé)
Iron, 3½ x 7½ x 4½″ (8.9 x 19.1 x 11.5 cm.)
Signed r. torso: *j. Gonzalez*
Collection The Baltimore Museum of Art: Gift of
Elinor Graham, Towson, Maryland (BMA 1978. 129)

Although there are published photographs of other sculptures of the same period and style (see Withers, p. 47, fig. 28), this *Reclining Figure* is one of the few pieces whose present whereabouts is known. The original owner of *Reclining Figure* was the artist and art dealer John Graham, who purchased it together with two other small sculptures directly from González in the early 1930s and was probably the sculptor's first American collector. Subsequently Graham gave one of the three sculptures, a mask, to Smith, who was fascinated by González's use of welding as a sculpture technique. Smith presumably had many opportunities to study the *Reclining Figure*, as he and his first wife Dorothy Dehner were close friends of the Grahams at that time. According to Dehner, in 1933, when he obtained blacksmith tools from a defunct shop in Ticonderoga, Smith created a small *Reclining Figure* in forged iron inspired by the González sculpture (fig.). In 1978 Graham's widow Elinor donated the sculpture to The Baltimore Museum of Art.

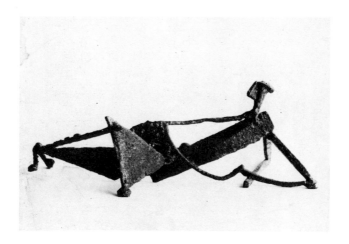

David Smith
Reclining Figure. 1933
Forged iron, 3¼ x 10½ x 5½″ (8.9 x 26.7 x 14 cm.)
Collection Dorothy Dehner, New York

89
Don Quixote. ca. 1929-30
(Don Quichotte)
Iron, 17¾″ (44 cm.) high
Signed l. back: *j. G.* Not dated.
Collection Musée National d'Art Moderne, Centre
Georges Pompidou, Paris, Don de Mme R. Gonzalez

REFERENCE:
Withers, p. 27, fig. 11, p. 158, no. 23

90a
Peasant Woman (with a Sickle). ca. 1929
(Paysanne)
Pencil and India ink on paper mounted on khaki
paper, drawing 9½ x 6⅛″ (24 x 15.5 cm.); mount
12⅜ x 9⅜″ (31.4 x 23.9 cm.)
Not signed or dated
Collection Carmen Martinez and Viviane
Grimminger, Paris

90b
Woman with a Broom. ca. 1929
(Femme au balai)
Pencil and India ink on tan cardboard mounted on
paper, drawing 9½ x 7¼″ (24.3 x 18.4 cm.); mount
11¼ x 8⅞″ (28.5 x 22.6 cm.)
Not signed or dated
Collection Carmen Martinez and Viviane
Grimminger, Paris
REFERENCES:
Gibert, vol. II, p. 192, repr.; vol. VI, p. 48, repr.

91
Woman with a Broom. ca. 1930
(Femme au balai)
Iron, 13 x 7¼ x 3½″ (33 x 18.5 x 8.9 cm.)
Signed on back of base: *J. Gonzalez* Not dated
Winston-Malbin Collection, New York
REFERENCE:
Withers, p. 159, no. 39

92

Woman with a Bundle of Sticks. ca. 1930-32
(Femme aux fagots)
Iron, 14⅜ x 5¾ x 4″ (36.6 x 14.6 x 10.2 cm.)
Signed and dated back r.: *j. Gonzalez / 1932*
Collection Hirshhorn Museum and Sculpture Garden, Smithsonian Institution, Washington, D.C.
REFERENCE:
Withers, p. 161, no. 53

González's early sculptures, incised and cut from plates of metal, show a figure-against-a-ground relationship that betrays their essentially pictorial vision and method. The artist would subsequently eliminate the background, but vestiges of it occasionally remained, as in *Woman with a Bundle of Sticks*. Contemporaneous drawings, such as *Peasant Woman with a Large Basket* (fig.), imply that what appears to be an abstract backdrop in this sculpture evokes in positive form the negative silhouette of an open door.

Woman with a Bundle of Sticks is signed and dated 1932. Yet its imagery and technique, more closely related to works of 1929-30, encourage speculation that it may have been executed at an earlier date.

González
Peasant Woman with a Large Basket. ca. 1929
Pencil, ink and wash on paper, 6¼ x 4¼″ (15.8 x 10.8 cm.)
Collection Carmen Martinez and Viviane Grimminger, Paris

93
Little Peasant Woman with a Hoe. ca. 1930
(Petite paysanne à la bêche)
Black and colored pencils and ink on cream paper,
6⅜ x 5⅜″ (16.2 x 13.6 cm.)
Not signed or dated
Private Collection

94
Two Standing Figures. ca. 1930
(Deux personnages debouts)
Pencil, ink and watercolor on paper, 9⅜ x 6¼″
(23.8 x 15.8 cm.)
Not signed or dated
Collection Museo de Arte Moderno, Barcelona, Gift
of Roberta González, 1972

REFERENCES:
Barcelona, p. 24, no. 99 (MAB 113.459)
Gibert, vol. VI, p. 71, repr.

95
Little Peasant Woman. ca. 1930-32
(Petite paysanne)
Silver, 6¾ x 2⅜ x 2⅛″ (17 x 6 x 5.5 cm.)
Not signed or dated
Collection Museo de Arte Moderno, Barcelona, Gift
of Roberta González, 1972

REFERENCES:
Barcelona, p. 18, no. 35, pl. 4 (MAB 113.440)
Withers, p. 163, no. 79

96a
Maternity Studies. ca. 1930
(Maternités)
Pencil, India ink and wash on paper, 9⅜ x 6¼″
(23.8 x 15.9 cm.)
Not signed or dated
Collection Carmen Martinez and Viviane
Grimminger, Paris

96b
Peasant Woman. 1931
(Paysanne)
Pencil and blue ink on paper, 6½ x 4⅝″
(16.5 x 11.3 cm.)
Signed and dated l.r.: *j. G./ 1931*
Collection Carmen Martinez and Viviane
Grimminger, Paris
REFERENCES:
Gibert, vol. III, p. 56, repr.; vol. II, p. 193, repr.

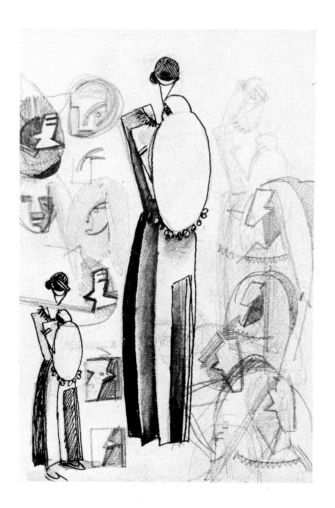

97
Woman "with Three Folds." ca. 1931
(Femme dite "aux trois plis")
Iron, 49¼ x 11 x 7⅛″ (125 x 28 x 18 cm.)
Not signed or dated
Collection Carmen Martinez and Viviane
Grimminger, Paris

REFERENCE:
Withers, p. 161, no. 52

98
Head Studies. ca. 1930
(Etudes de têtes)
Pencil on paper, 6⅛ x 7¾″ (15.4 x 19.8 cm.)
Not signed or dated
Courtesy The Pace Gallery, New York

REFERENCE:
Gibert, vol. VIII, p. 109, repr.

99
Small Cutout Mask. ca. 1930
(Petit masque decoupé)
Pencil on paper mounted on dark green paper,
drawing 4 x 2⅛″ (10.2 x 5.4 cm.); mount 7⅞ x 5″
(20 x 12.5 cm.)
Not signed or dated
Collection Carmen Martinez and Viviane
Grimminger, Paris

REFERENCE:
Gibert, vol. VIII, p. 21, repr.

100
Head Called "The Rabbit." ca. 1930
(Tête dite "Le Lapin")
Iron, 13¼ x 7⅛ x 4⅜″ (33.5 x 14 x 11 cm.)
Not signed or dated
Collection Museo Español de Arte Contemporáneo,
Madrid (Donación Roberta González)

REFERENCES:
Madrid, p. 147 (E-472)
Withers, p. 160, no. 46

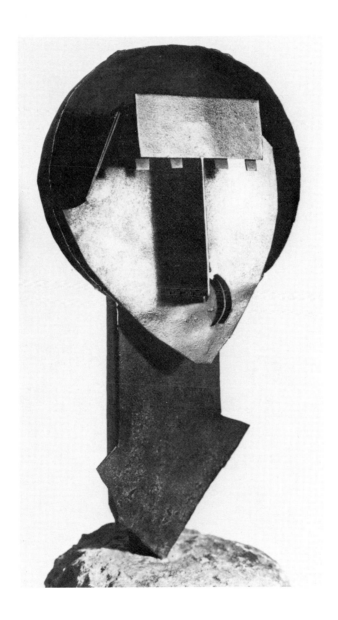

101
Head of a Woman I (Head of Uncle Joan I).
ca. 1930
(Tête de femme I [Tête d'oncle Jean I])
Iron, 10¾ x 6½" (27.4 x 16.5 cm.)
Not signed or dated
Collection Museo de Arte Moderno, Barcelona, Gift
of Roberta González, 1972
REFERENCES:
Barcelona, p. 15, no. 8 (MAB 113.437)
Withers, p. 160, no. 42

102
Head of a Woman II (Head of Uncle Joan II).
ca. 1930
(Tête de femme II [Tête d'oncle Jean II])
Iron, 14⅞ x 6½ x 4⅛″ (37.9 x 16.4 x 10.5 cm.)
Signed on base plate: *j. Gonzalez*
Collection Hans Hartung, Antibes

REFERENCE:
Withers, p. 160, no. 43

The visual affinities of the two heads traditionally named *Tête d'Oncle Jean I* and *II* to other sculptures and drawings of ca. 1930 lead us to question their identification as masculine portraits. On the contrary, the ring of metal that encircles the head was used frequently during this period by González and usually signified the edge of a woman's scarf or hat, and the zigzag at the base of the neck probably refers to a lace-collared neckline.

The "Joan" traditionally cited, González's brother and therefore his daughter Roberta's uncle, died in 1908; Roberta never knew him. We may assume that these titles were chosen by Roberta based on somewhat precarious distant memories.

103
Head with Large Eyes. ca. 1930
(Tête aux grands yeux)
Iron, 13¼ x 7¼ x 6½″ (33.7 x 18.5 x 16.5 cm.)
Not signed or dated
Collection Wilhelm Lehmbruck Museum, Duisberg

REFERENCE:
Withers, p. 51, fig. 36, p. 160, no. 48

104
Head in Depth. 1930
(Tête en profondeur)
Iron, 10¼ x 8 x 6⅜″ (26 x 20.1 x 16.1 cm.)
Signed and dated on back c.l.: *j. Gonzalez / 1930*
Collection Hans Hartung, Antibes

REFERENCE:
Withers, p. 50, fig. 34, p. 160, no. 41

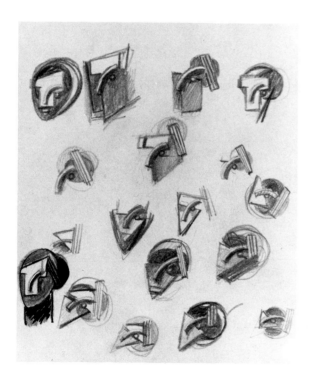

105a
Studies Related to "Head in Depth" and "Head with Chignon." 1931
(Etudes en rapport avec "Tête en profondeur" et "Tête au chignon")
Pencil and ink on paper, 6⅜ x 5¼″ (17.2 x 13.4 cm.)
Not signed or dated
Collection The Solomon R. Guggenheim Museum, New York

105b
Studies Related to "Head in Depth" and "Head with Chignon." 1931
(Etudes en rapport avec "Tête en profondeur" et "Tête au chignon")
Pencil and ink on paper, 6⅜ x 5¼″ (17.2 x 13.4 cm.)
Not signed or dated
Collection The Solomon R. Guggenheim Museum, New York

106
Head with Chignon. ca. 1930
(Tête au chignon)
Iron, including base 21½″ (54.1 cm.) high
Not signed or dated
Lent by The Art Institute of Chicago, The Ada
Turnbull Hertle Fund Income, Laura R. Magnuson
Fund Income, Samuel A. Marx Fund Income and
Morris L. Parker Fund
REFERENCE:
Withers, p. 160, no. 47

107a
Strange Mask. ca. 1930
(Masque étrange)
Pencil and India ink on textured cardboard,
3⅛ x 3½″ (8 x 8.8 cm.)
Not signed or dated
Collection Carmen Martinez and Viviane
Grimminger, Paris

107b
Double Face. ca. 1930
(Double visage)
Pencil and India ink on textured cardboard,
1¾ x 2⅛″ (4.4 x 5.5 cm.)
Not signed or dated
Collection Carmen Martinez and Viviane
Grimminger, Paris

107c
Study for "The Kiss," No. 1. ca. 1930
(Etude pour "Le Baiser," no. 1)
India ink on textured cardboard, 2 x 2½″
(5.2 x 6.5 cm.)
Not signed or dated
Collection Carmen Martinez and Viviane
Grimminger, Paris

107d
Study for "The Kiss," No. 3. ca. 1930
(Etude pour "Le Baiser," no. 3)
Pencil and India ink on textured cardboard,
3⅛ x 3¼″ (8 x 8.4 cm.)
Not signed or dated
Collection Carmen Martinez and Viviane
Grimminger, Paris

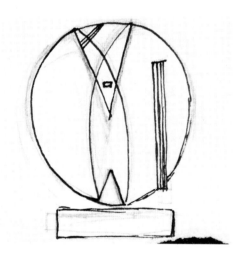

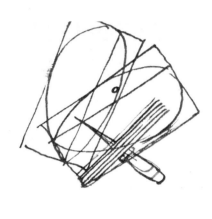

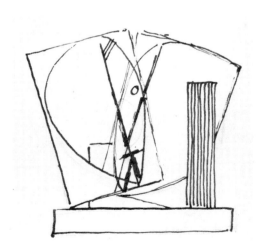

107e
Study for "The Kiss," No. 5. ca. 1930
(Etude pour "Le Baiser," no. 5)
Pencil and India ink on textured cardboard,
3⅛ x 2⅞" (8 x 7.4 cm.)
Not signed or dated
Collection Carmen Martinez and Viviane
Grimminger, Paris

107f
Study for "The Kiss," No. 2. ca. 1930
(Etude pour "Le Baiser," no. 2)
Pencil and India ink on textured cardboard,
5⅛ x 5⅜" (13 x 13.7 cm.)
Not signed or dated
Collection Carmen Martinez and Viviane
Grimminger, Paris

107g
Study for "The Kiss," No. 4. ca. 1930
(Etude pour "Le Baiser," no. 4)
India ink on cream cardboard, 3⅛ x 3¾"
(8 x 9.4 cm.)
Not signed or dated
Collection Carmen Martinez and Viviane
Grimminger, Paris

REFERENCES:
Gibert, vol. VIII, pp. 30-33, reprs.

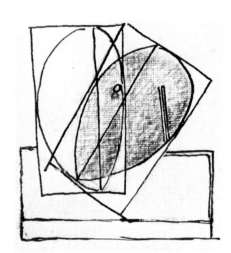

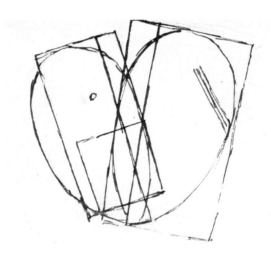

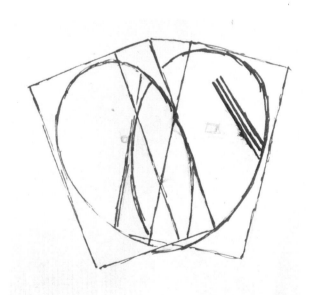

108
Study After "The Kiss." 1935
(Etude d'après "Le Baiser")
Pencil, ink and oil pastel on paper, 6⅞ x 5¼″
(17.6 x 13.3 cm.)
Signed and dated l.r.: *j.G. | 1935*
The Arthur and Madeleine Lejwa Collection,
New York

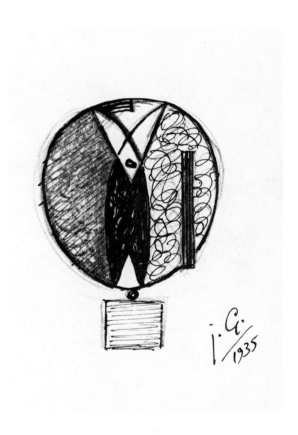

109
The Kiss. ca. 1930
(Le Baiser)
Iron, 10½ x 11¼ x 3″ (26.7 x 28.5 x 7.6 cm.)
Signed and dated on back u.l.: *j. Gonzalez / 1930*
Winston-Malbin Collection, New York

REFERENCE:
Withers, p. 51, fig. 35, p. 159, no. 34

110
Head. ca. 1930
(Tête)
Pencil on textured cardboard mounted on dark gray
paper, drawing, irregular, ca. 2¾ x 2½″ (7 x 6.4
cm.); mount 10⅝ x 8¼″ (27 x 21 cm.)
Not signed or dated
Collection The Solomon R. Guggenheim Museum,
Gift of Carmen Martinez and Viviane Grimminger
REFERENCE:
Gibert, vol. VIII, p. 21, repr.

111
"Science-Fiction" Heads. ca. 1930
(Têtes "science-fiction")
Pencil, ink and wash on paper, 10 x 6⅝″
(25.5 x 16.8 cm.)
Not signed or dated
Courtesy Galerie Beyeler, Basel
REFERENCE:
Gibert, vol. VIII, p. 29, repr.

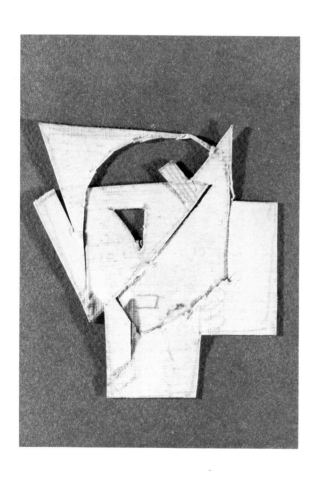

112
Harlequin. Pierrot. 1930-31
(Arlequin. Pierrot)
Iron, 17 x 11⅞ x 11⅞" (43 x 30 x 30 cm.)
Signed on base plate l.r.: *j. G.* Not dated
Collection Kunsthaus Zürich

REFERENCE:
Withers, p. 40, fig. 17, p. 159, no. 33

113
Young Woman Fixing Her Hair. 1924
(Jeune femme se coiffant)
Pencil on paper, 10 x 6½″ (25.4 x 16.5 cm.)
Signed and dated l.r.: *j. G. / 1924*
Collection Carmen Martinez and Viviane
Grimminger, Paris

114
Nude Fixing Her Hair. 1928
(Nu se coiffant)
Pencil and blue ink on paper, 9⅞ x 6¼″
(25 x 16 cm.)
Signed and dated l.r.: *J. Gonzalez / 1928*
Private Collection

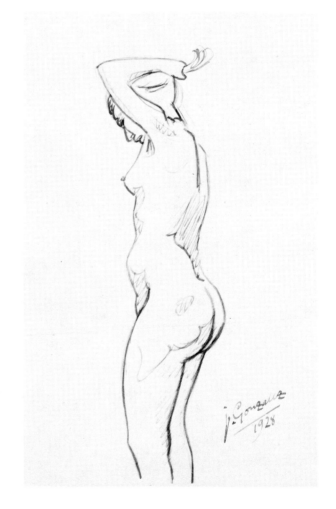

115
Woman Combing Her Hair. ca. 1928
(Femme se coiffant)
Pencil on paper, 11¾ x 7⅞″ (29.8 x 20 cm.)
Not signed or dated
Private Collection

116
Woman Dressing (Fixing Her Hair). ca. 1929
(Femme s'habillant)
Ink and watercolor on paper, 6⅞ x 6¼″
(17.7 x 15.8 cm.)
Not signed or dated
Collection Carmen Martinez and Viviane
Grimminger, Paris

REFERENCE:
Gibert, vol. V, p. 41, repr.

117a
Study for "Woman Combing Her Hair." ca. 1930
(Etude pour "Femme se coiffant")
Colored pencil on paper, 6⅜ x 5⅜″ (16.3 x 13.6 cm.)
Not signed or dated
Private Collection

117b
Study for "Woman Combing Her Hair." ca. 1930
(Etude pour "Femme se coiffant")
Pencil on paper, 6⅜ x 5⅜″ (16.3 x 13.6 cm.)
Not signed or dated
Private Collection

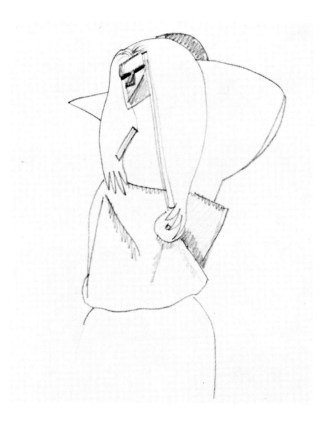

Study for "Woman Combing Her Hair." ca. 1930
(Etude pour "Femme se coiffant")

117c
Head Studies for "Woman Combing Her Hair."
ca. 1930
(Etude de têtes pour "Femme se coiffant")
Colored pencil on paper, 6⅜ x 5⅜″ (16.3 x 13.6 cm.)
Not signed or dated
Private Collection

118a
Study for "Woman Combing Her Hair," No. 2.
ca. 1930-31
(Etude pour "Femme se coiffant," no. 2)
Black and colored pencils and India ink on beige
paper, 6⅜ x 5⅜″ (16.2 x 13.5 cm.)
Not signed or dated
Collection Carmen Martinez and Viviane
Grimminger, Paris

118b
Study for "Woman Combing Her Hair," No. 4.
ca. 1930-31
(Etude pour "Femme se coiffant," no. 4)
Black and colored pencils and India ink on beige
paper, 6⅜ x 5⅜″ (16.2 x 13.5 cm.)
Not signed or dated
Collection Carmen Martinez and Viviane
Grimminger, Paris

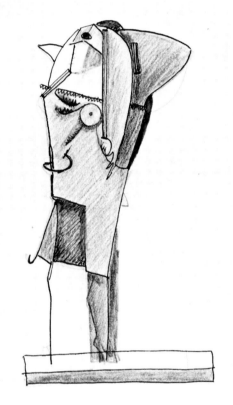

118c
Study for "Woman Combing Her Hair," No. 8.
ca. 1930-31
(Etude pour "Femme se coiffant," no. 8)
Black and colored pencils on paper, 6½ x 4⅜"
(16.5 x 11.2 cm.)
Not signed or dated
Collection Carmen Martinez and Viviane
Grimminger, Paris

REFERENCES:
Gibert, vol. V, pp. 44, 45, 47, reprs.

119
Study for "Woman Combing Her Hair." ca. 1930-31
(Etude pour "Femme se coiffant")
Black and colored pencils, blue and India ink on
paper, 6½ x 4½" (16.6 x 11.5 cm.)
Not signed or dated
Collection The Solomon R. Guggenheim Museum,
New York, Gift of Carmen Martinez and Viviane
Grimminger

REFERENCE:
Gibert, vol. V, p. 48, repr.

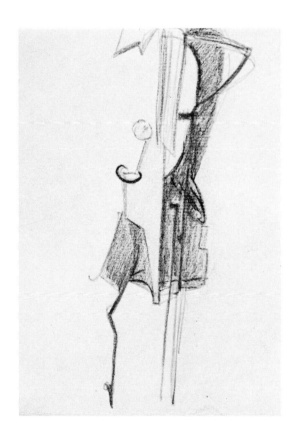

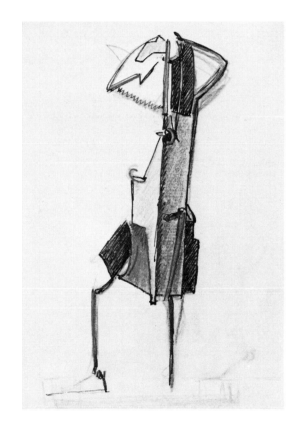

120
Woman Combing Her Hair. ca. 1931
(Femme se coiffant)
Iron, 67 x 21¾ x 7⅞″ (170 x 55 x 20 cm.)
Not signed or dated
Collection Musée National d'Art Moderne, Centre
Georges Pompidou, Paris, Don de Mme R. Gonzalez
REFERENCE:
Withers, p. 54, fig. 37, p. 160, no. 51

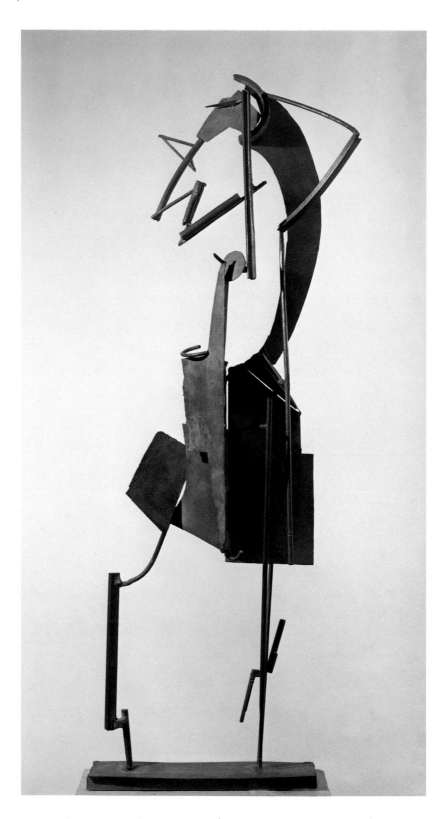

121
Head of a Harlequin. 1932
(Tête d'arlequin)
Iron, 10½ x 6⅞ x 5½″ (26.7 x 17.4 x 14 cm.)
Signed and dated on back l.r.: *j. Gonzalez / 1932*
Collection Estate of Joaquín Torres-García

122
The Lovers I. ca. 1932
(Les Amoureux I)
Iron, 7 x 3¾ x 3⅜″ (17.8 x 9.5 x 8.5 cm.)
Not signed or dated
Collection Carmen Martinez and Viviane
Grimminger, Paris
REFERENCE:
Withers, p. 162, no. 65

123
The Lovers II. ca. 1932
(Les Amoureux II)
Iron, 18 x 9 x 6½″ (45.7 x 22.9 x 16.5 cm.)
Not signed or dated
Collection Carmen Martinez and Viviane
Grimminger, Paris
REFERENCE:
Withers, p. 58, fig. 46, p. 162, no. 66

124
Mask, Light and Shadow. ca. 1932
(Masque, ombre et lumière)
Iron, 11 x 4″ (28 x 10 cm.)
Not signed or dated
Private Collection

125
Resplendence (Standing Figure). 1932
(Eblouissement [Personnage debout])
Silver, 8¼″ (21 cm.) high
Signed and dated on back l.c.: *j. Gonzalez* / *1932*
Philadelphia Museum of Art, A. E. Gallatin
Collection

REFERENCE:
Withers, p. 58, fig. 47, p. 161, no. 60

This small silver sculpture was purchased by A. E.
Gallatin directly from González sometime between
August 16 and 24, 1935, according to letters in the
González Estate Archive. It was one of the earliest
pieces that the sculptor sold to an important collector. In a note from the Hotel Georges V in Paris
dated August 24, Gallatin asked González for the
title of the sculpture he had purchased. González
scribbled on the note: *"répondu le 2-9-35 'Eblouisse-*
ment.'" (González Estate Archive, Paris)

The theme of this work is possibly a Woman Combing Her Hair, in a stage somewhere between the Paris
version of ca. 1931 (cat. no. 120) and the Stockholm
version of ca. 1934 (cat. no. 149).

126
Small Head. ca. 1932
(Petite tête)
Silver, 5⅛ x 2⅜ x 2⅜″ (13 x 6 x 6 cm.)
Not signed or dated
Collection Museo Español de Arte Contemporáneo,
Madrid (Donación Roberta González)

REFERENCES:
Madrid, p. 148 (E-446)
Withers, p. 60, fig. 51, pp. 161-162, no. 62

127
Study after "Small Head." 1935
(Etude d'apres "Petite Tête")
Pencil, ink and oil pastel on paper, 6¾ x 5¼″
(17.3 x 13.4 cm.)
Signed and dated l.l.: *j. G. / 1935*
Private Collection

128
Study Related to "The Dream." 1933
(Etude d'après "Le Rêve")
Colored pencil, India ink and wash on ivory paper,
9⅝ x 5⅝″ (24.3 x 14.4 cm.)
Signed and dated l.r.: *2-2-33 / j. G.*
Private Collection

REFERENCE:
Gibert, vol. VIII, p. 37

129
Head Called "The Large Trumpet." ca. 1932-33
(Tête dite "La Grande trompette")
Iron, 38⅝″ (98 cm.) high
Not signed or dated
Collection Dr. W. A. Bechtler, Zollikon
REFERENCE:
Withers, p. 56, fig. 42, p. 161, no. 56

130
The Dream, The Kiss. ca. 1932-33
(Le Rêve, Le Baiser)
Iron, 26⅜ x 11⅞ x 9¼″ (67 x 30 x 23.5 cm.)
Not signed or dated
Collection Musée National d'Art Moderne, Centre
Georges Pompidou, Paris, Legs R. Gonzalez
REFERENCE:
Withers, p. 55, fig. 40, p. 161, no. 54

131
Head on a Long Stalk. ca. 1932-33
(Tête longue tige)
Iron, 23⅝ x 8⅝ x 5⅛″ (60 x 22 x 13 cm.)
Not signed or dated.
Courtesy David Grob, London
REFERENCE:
Withers, p. 58, fig. 48, p. 161, no. 59

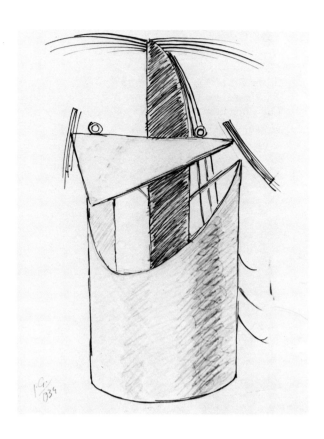

132
Imaginary Head. 1934
(Visage fantastique)
Black and colored pencils and ink on paper,
12¾ x 9⅞″ (32.5 x 25.1 cm.)
Signed and dated l.l.: *j.G. /1934*
Collection The Trustees of the Tate Gallery, London
REFERENCES:
Tate, p. 314, repr. (T. 1605)
Gibert, vol. VIII, p. 43, repr.

133
Study Related to "Head Called 'The Fireman.' "
1934
(Etude en rapport avec "Tête dite 'Le Pompier' ")
Colored pencil and ink on paper, 7⅛ x 4″
(18 x 10 cm.)
Signed and dated l.r.: *j. G. | 1934*
Private Collection

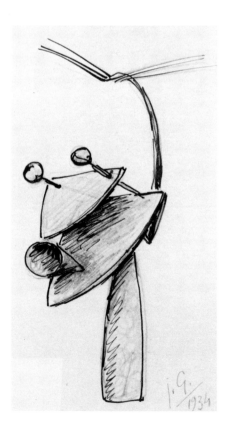

134
Small Head with Triangle. ca. 1933
(Petite tête au triangle)
Silver, 9⅛ x 2⅞ x 3¾″ (23.1 x 7.3 x 9.6 cm.)
Not signed or dated
Collection Hans Hartung, Antibes

REFERENCE:
Withers, p. 59, fig. 50, p. 161, no. 61

135
Head Called "The Fireman." ca. 1933
(Tête dite "Le Pompier")
Silver, 5⅜ x 2⅜ x 3⅛″ (13.6 x 5.5 x 8 cm.)
Not signed or dated
Collection Branco Weiss, Zürich

REFERENCE:
Withers, p. 59, fig. 49, p. 162, no. 63

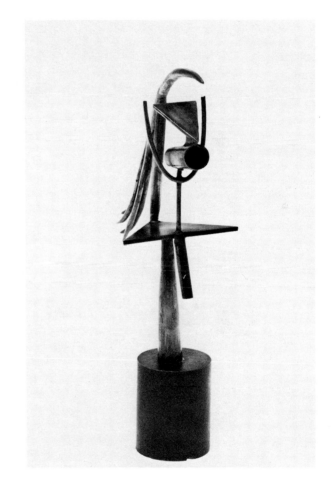

136
Mane of Hair. ca. 1934
(La Chevelure)
Forged bronze, 11⅜ x 6¾ x 8⅝″ (29 x 17 x 22 cm.)
Not signed or dated
Courtesy Galerie de France, Paris

137
Head with Mirror. ca. 1934
(Tête au miroir)
Forged bronze, 23½ x 11⅝ x 13⅞"
(59.5 x 29.5 x 35 cm.)
Not signed or dated
Collection Association Fondation Christian et
Yvonne Zervos, Vézelay
REFERENCE:
Withers, p. 69, fig. 71, p. 163, no. 80

138
Head Called "The Swiss Woman." ca. 1934
(Tête dite "La Suissesse")
Iron, 15 x 8¼ x 7½" (38 x 21 x 19 cm.)
Not signed or dated
Collection Kunsthalle Bielefeld
REFERENCE:
Withers, p. 55, fig. 41, p. 161, no. 55

139
Head with Three Verticals. 1934
(Tête aux trois verticales)
Black and colored pencils and India ink on paper,
12⅝ x 9⅝" (32.1 x 24.5 cm.)
Signed and dated l.r.: *j. G. / 1934*
Private Collection
REFERENCE:
Gibert, vol. VIII, p. 41, repr.

140
Sharply Pointed Head. 1934
(Tête acérée)
Black and colored pencils and India ink on paper,
9⅝ x 10⅞" (24.5 x 25 cm.)
Signed and dated l.l.: *j. G. / 1934*
Private Collection
REFERENCE:
Gibert, vol. VIII, p. 41, repr.

141
Study for "Maternity." 1934
(Etude pour "La Maternité")
Black and colored pencils and ink on cream paper,
9⅝ x 6¼" (24.6 x 15.9 cm.)
Signed and dated l.r.: *j.G. / 1934*
Collection The Trustees of the Tate Gallery, London
REFERENCES:
Tate, p. 314, repr. (T. 1500)
Gibert, vol. III, p. 70, repr.

142
Study for "Small Maternity." 1934
(Etude pour "Petite maternité")
Pencil and ink on paper, 9½ x 3¾" (24 x 9.5 cm.)
Signed and dated l.r.: *j.G. / 1934*
Collection Staatsgalerie Stuttgart

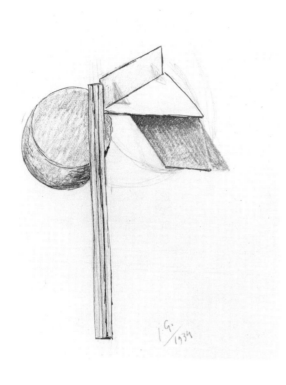

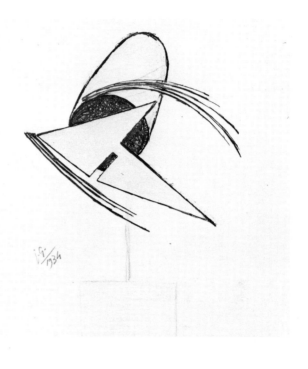

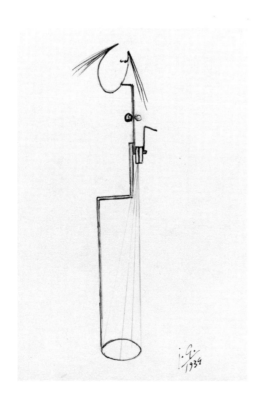

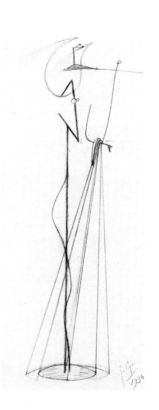

143
Head Called "The Tunnel." ca. 1934
(Tête dite "Le Tunnel")
Iron, 18⅜ x 8½ x 12⅛″ (46.7 x 21.8 x 30.9 cm.)
Not signed or dated
Collection The Trustees of the Tate Gallery, London

REFERENCES:
Tate, p. 313, repr. (T. 1698)
Withers, p. 57, fig. 44, p. 162, no. 71

144
Figure Called "Woman with a Mirror." ca. 1934
(Personnage dit "La Femme au miroir")
Iron, 20¼ x 4⅞ x 5½" (51.5 x 12.5 x 14 cm.)
Not signed or dated
Courtesy Galerie de France, Paris

145
*"Science-Fiction" Figure (Study for "Woman
Combing Her Hair.")* 1934
(Personnage "Science-fiction")
Colored pencil and India ink on paper, 6¼ x 5⅜″
(16 x 13.5 cm.)
Signed and dated l.r.: *j.G. / 1934*
Collection Museo Español de Arte Contemporáneo,
Madrid (Donación Roberta González)

REFERENCES:
Madrid, p. 173 (D-429)
Gibert, vol. IX, p. 10, repr.

146
Study for "Woman Combing Her Hair." 1934
(Etude pour "Femme se coiffant")
Ink and crayon on paper, 9½ x 5½″ (24 x 14 cm.)
Signed and dated l.r.: *j. G. / 1934*
Collection Moderna Museet, Stockholm

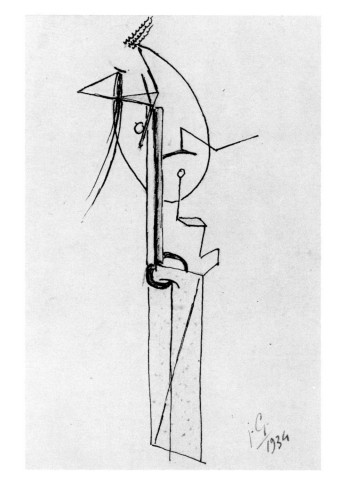

147
Study for "Woman Combing Her Hair." 1934
(Etude pour "Femme se coiffant")
Ink and crayon on paper, 9½ x 5¾″ (24 x 14.5 cm.)
Signed and dated l.r.: *j.G.* / *1934*
Collection Moderna Museet, Stockholm

148
Study for "Woman Combing Her Hair." 1934
(Etude pour "Femme se coiffant")
Ink and crayon on paper, 9½ x 5⅞″ (24 x 15 cm.)
Signed and dated l.r.: *j. G.* / *1934*
Collection Moderna Museet, Stockholm

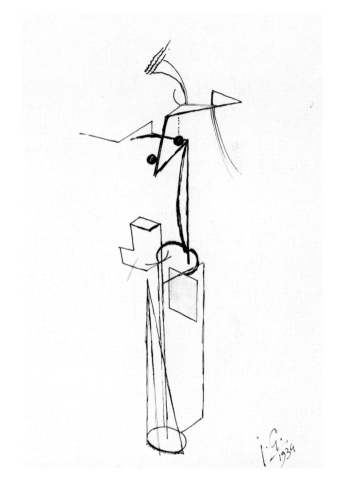

149
Woman Combing Her Hair. ca. 1934
(Femme se coiffant)
Iron, 47¾″ (121 cm.) high
Not signed or dated
Collection Moderna Museet, Stockholm

REFERENCE:
Withers, p. 62, fig. 55, p. 164, no. 86

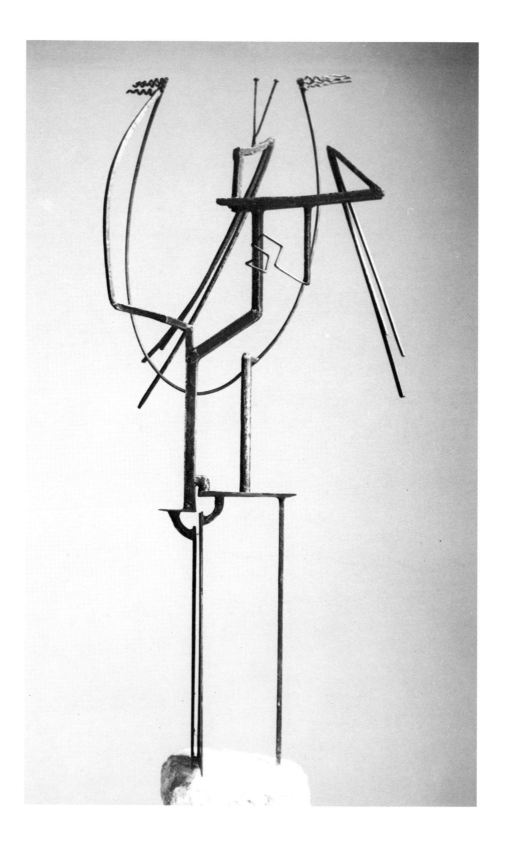

150
Small Dancer. ca. 1935
(Petite danseuse)
Iron, 7 x 4 x 1⅛″ (17.7 x 10 x 4 cm.)
Not signed or dated
Collection Musée National d'Art Moderne, Centre
Georges Pompidou, Paris, Don de Mme R. Gonzalez
REFERENCE:
Withers, p. 85, fig. 101, p. 164, no. 91

151
Dancer with Flying Hair. ca. 1935
(Danseuse échévelée)
Iron, 24⅜″ (62 cm.) high
Not signed or dated
Don Gildas Fardel, Centre de Documentation
Internationale d'art contemporain. Musée des
Beaux-Arts de Nantes
REFERENCE:
Withers, p. 164, no. 89

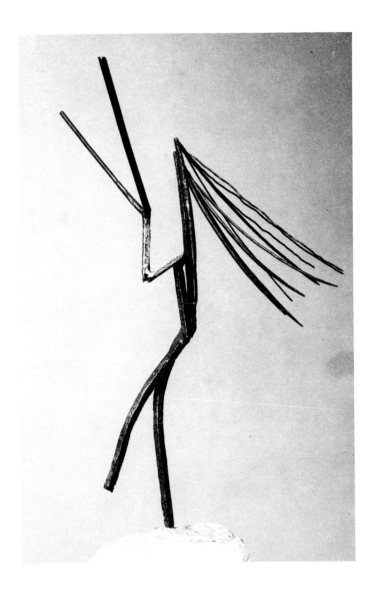

152
Study After "Large Standing Figure." 1935
(Etude d'après "Personnage debout")
Pencil, ink and wax crayon on paper, 12¼ x 9¼″
(31.3 x 23.8 cm.)
Signed and dated l.r.: *j.G. / 1937-36 / 24–3*
The Arthur and Madeleine Lejwa Collection,
New York

REFERENCE:
Gibert, vol. IX, p. 53, repr.

153
Yellow and White Standing Figure. 1937
(Personnage debout jaune et blanc)
India ink, wax crayon and collage on green paper,
12¾ x 9⅞″ (32.5 x 25 cm.)
Signed and dated l.l.: *j.G. / 1937 / 31–3*
Collection Museo Español de Arte Contemporáneo,
Madrid (Donación Roberta González)

REFERENCES:
Madrid, p. 172 (D-423)
Gibert, vol. IX, p. 54, repr.

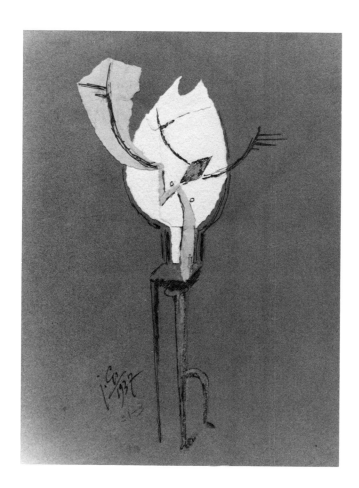

154
Large Standing Figure. ca. 1935
(Grand personnage debout)
Iron, 50⅜ x 27¼ x 15¾″ (128 x 69 x 40 cm.)
Not signed or dated
Collection Fondation Maeght, Saint-Paul-de-Vence,
France

REFERENCES:
Maeght, p. 5, repr., p. 29, no. 1
Withers, p. 67, fig. 68, pp. 164-165, no. 92

155
Study Related to Various Sculptures. 1935
(Etudes en rapport avec sculptures diverses)
Pencil, India ink and wax crayon on paper,
9½ x 6⅛″ (24 x 15.6 cm.)
Signed and dated l.r.: *j. G. / 1935*; inscribed l.c.: *3*
Collection Carmen Martinez and Viviane
Grimminger, Paris

156
The Angel. The Insect. Dancer. ca. 1935
(L'Ange. L'Insecte. Danseuse)
Iron, 64¼ x 18⅛ x 12⅝" (163 x 46 x 32 cm.)
Not signed or dated
Collection Musée National d'Art Moderne, Centre
Georges Pompidou, Paris

REFERENCE:
Withers, p. 70, fig. 74, p. 165, no. 94

157
Study After "Daphne." 1937
(Etude d'après "Daphné")
Black and colored pencils, ink and wash on blue
paper, 9⅞ x 6⅜″ (25 x 16.3 cm.)
Signed and dated l.l.: *j.G. / 1937 / 8–2*; inscribed
l.r: DAPHNE
Courtesy Galerie Beyeler, Basel

REFERENCE:
Gibert, vol. IX, p. 44, repr.

158
Figure with a White Rectangle. 1937
(Personnage au rectangle blanc)
Pencil, ink and collage on green paper, 12⅞ x 10″
(32.6 x 25.3 cm.)
Signed and dated l.l.: *j.G. / 1937 / 4–4*
Collection The Trustees of the Tate Gallery, London

REFERENCES:
Tate, p. 318, repr. (T. 1612)
Gibert, vol. IX, p. 46, repr.

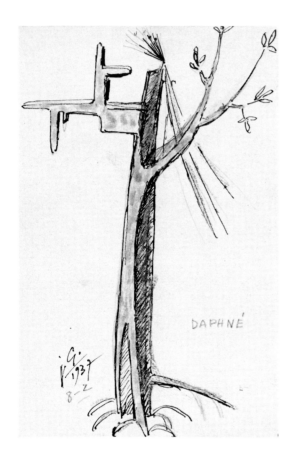

159
Daphne. ca. 1935
(Daphné)
Iron, 55⅞″ (142 cm.) high
Not signed or dated
Collection Dr. W. A. Bechtler, Zollikon

REFERENCE:
Withers, p. 61, figs. 53, 54, p. 163, no. 81

160
Vibrating Figure. 1936
(Personnage vibrant)
India ink, gouache and wax crayon with traces of
pencil on paper, 12⅝ x 9½″ (32 x 24 cm.)
Signed and dated l.l.: *j. G.* / *2–9 1936*
Collection The Solomon R. Guggenheim Museum,
New York, Gift of Carmen Martinez and Viviane
Grimminger

REFERENCE:
Gibert, vol. IX, p. 30, repr.

161
Figure with Large Circle. 1936
(Personnage dit au grand cercle)
India ink and gouache on paper, 8⅞ x 6⅛″
(22.5 x 15.7 cm.)
Signed and dated l.l.: *j. G.* / *19–9 1936*
Collection Carmen Martinez and Viviane
Grimminger, Paris

REFERENCE:
Gibert, vol. IX, p. 35, repr.

162
Figure Called "The Giraffe." ca. 1935
(Personnage dit "La Girafe")
Iron, 37⅜ x 7⅛″ (95 x 18 cm.)
Not signed or dated
Collection Musée National d'Art Moderne, Centre
Georges Pompidou, Paris

REFERENCE:
Withers, p. 77, fig. 81, p. 165, no. 96

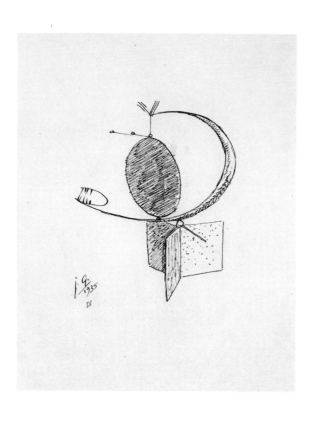

163
Study for "Head." 1935
(Etude pour "Tête")
Pencil and ink on paper, 12½ x 9⅝"
(31.5 x 24.2 cm.)
Signed, dated and inscribed l.l.: *j.G. / 1935 / IV*
Collection The Museum of Modern Art, New York,
Gift of Roberta González-Richard
REFERENCE:
Gibert, vol. VIII, p. 51, repr.

164
Study for "Head." 1936
(Etude pour "Tête")
Ink, gouache, wax crayon and collage on paper,
11 x 7½" (27.9 x 18.9 cm.)
Signed and dated l.c.: *j. G. / 1936*
Collection The Museum of Modern Art, New York,
Gift of Dr. and Mrs. Arthur Lejwa
REFERENCE:
Gibert, vol. VIII, p. 57, repr.

165
Study for a Sculpture. 1935
(Etude pour une sculpture)
Colored pencil, ink and pastel on paper, 9⅞ x 6¾"
(25 x 17.2 cm.)
Signed and dated l.l.: *j.G. / 1935*
Collection Carmen Martinez and Viviane
Grimminger, Paris

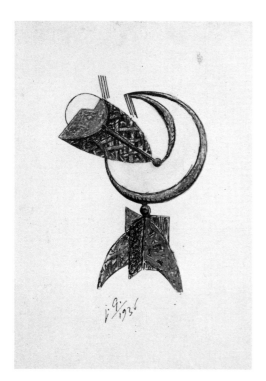

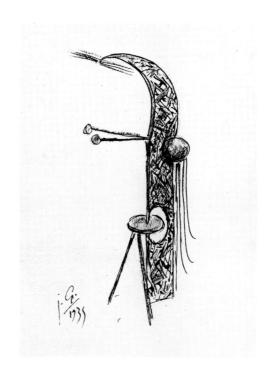

166
Head. The Snail. ca. 1935
(Tête. L'Escargot)
Iron, 17¾ x 15¼″ (45 x 38.7 cm.)
Not signed or dated
Collection The Museum of Modern Art, New York,
Purchase, 1937

REFERENCE:
Withers, p. 69, fig. 73, p. 165, no. 95

167
Seated Woman. 1935
(Femme assise)
Pencil and ink on paper, 5¾ x 5″ (14.5 x 12.5 cm.)
Signed and dated l.l.: *j. G. / 1935*
Courtesy Galerie de France, Paris

168
Study for "Seated Woman I." 1935
(Etude pour "Femme assise I")
Ink, wax crayon and oil pastel on paper, 10½ x 6″
(26.5 x 15.2 cm.)
Signed and dated l.l.: *j. G. / 1935 / 6 fois*
Collection Carmen Martinez and Viviane
Grimminger, Paris

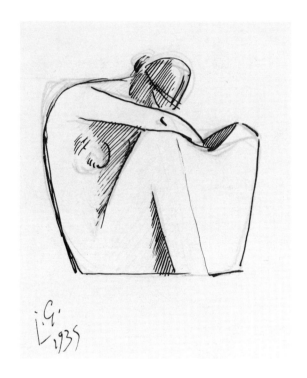

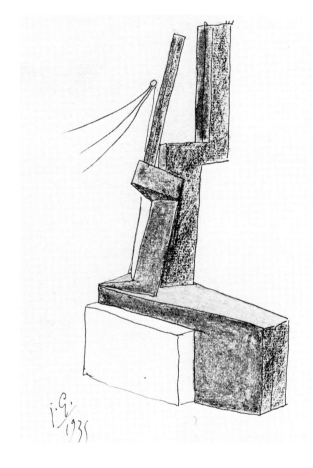

169a
Study for "Seated Woman I." 1935
(Etude pour "Femme assise I")
Ink and pastel on paper, 9½ x 6″ (24.2 x 15.3 cm.)
Signed and dated l.l.: *j.G. / 1935*
Courtesy The Pace Gallery, New York

169b
Study for "Seated Woman I." 1935
(Etude pour "Femme assise I")
Ink and pastel on paper, 9¼ x 6″ (23.2 x 15.3 cm.)
Signed and dated l.l.: *j.G. / 1935*
Courtesy The Pace Gallery, New York

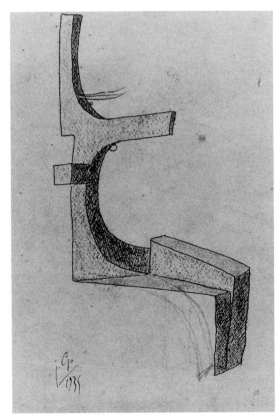

170
Seated Woman I. ca. 1935
(Femme assise I)
Iron, 46½ x 21¼ x 14¼″ (118 x 54 x 36 cm.)
Not signed or dated
Collection Carmen Martinez and Viviane
Grimminger, Paris
REFERENCE:
Withers, p. 77, fig. 80, p. 165, no. 97

171
Seated Pensive Woman. 1936
(Femme assise pensive)
Pencil, India ink, wax crayon and oil pastel on
paper, 6¼ x 5⅛″ (15.8 x 13.1 cm.)
Signed and dated l.l.: *j. G./ 1936*
Collection Carmen Martinez and Viviane
Grimminger, Paris

REFERENCE:
Gibert, vol. IV, p. 101, repr.

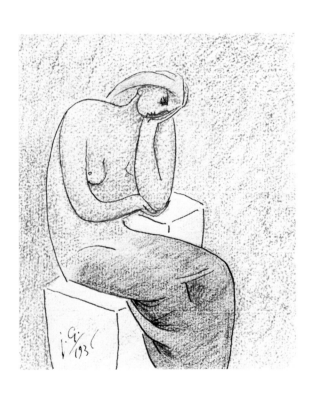

172
Seated Headless Nude in Profile. 1936
(Nu assis de profil sans tête)
India ink on paper, 6 x 9⅝″ (15.2 x 24.5 cm.)
Signed and dated l.l.: *j. G./ 1936*
Collection Carmen Martinez and Viviane
Grimminger, Paris
REFERENCE:
Gibert, vol. IV, p. 112, repr.

173
Standing Nude. 1936
(Nu debout)
India ink on paper, 9⅜ x 6⅜″ (23.8 x 16 cm.)
Signed and dated l.r.: *j.G. / 1936*
Courtesy Galerie Beyeler, Basel

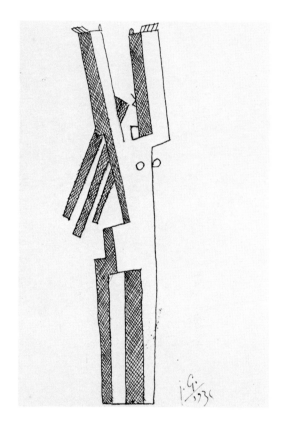

174
Seated Woman II. ca. 1936
(Femme assise II)
Iron, 33⅞ x 14⅝ x 9⅞″ (86 x 37 x 25 cm.)
Not signed or dated
Collection Musée National d'Art Moderne, Centre
Georges Pompidou, Paris, Legs Mme R. Gonzalez

REFERENCE:
Withers, p. 95, fig. 123, p. 165, no. 98

175
Head with Long Neck. 1936
(Tête long cou)
India ink and wax crayon on paper, 9½ x 5¼″
(24.1 x 13.3 cm.)
Signed and dated l.l.: *j. G.* / *1936*
Collection the Fogg Art Museum, Harvard University, Cambridge, Massachusetts, Gift—Catherine B. Freedberg, in honor of Roberta González

REFERENCE:
Gibert, vol. VIII, p. 63, repr.

176
Architectural Head. 1936
(Tête architecturée)
India ink and wax crayon with traces of pencil on paper, 6¼ x 8¼″ (15.7 x 20.7 cm.)
Signed and dated l.l.: *j.G.* / *1936*
Collection The Solomon R. Guggenheim Museum, New York, Gift of Carmen Martinez and Viviane Grimminger

REFERENCE:
Gibert, vol. VIII, p. 60, repr.

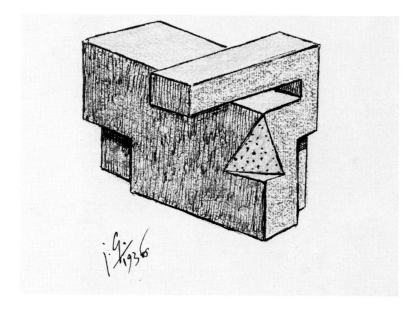

177

Two-dimensional Head Called "The Kiss." ca. 1936
(Tête plate dite "Le Baiser")
Stone, 10 x 8¼ x 2⅜″ (25.4 x 21 x 6 cm.)
Not signed or dated
Collection Carmen Martinez and Viviane
Grimminger, Paris

REFERENCE:
Withers, p. 78, fig. 84, p. 166, no. 106

178
Sulky Face. 1936
(Visage boudeur)
Pencil, ink and watercolor on paper, 12⅛ x 9⅛″
(30.7 x 23.2 cm.)
Signed and dated l.l.: *j.G. / 1936 / 26–12*
Collection The Trustees of the Tate Gallery, London

REFERENCES:
Tate, p. 317, repr. (T. 1606)
Gibert, vol. VIII, p. 89, repr.

179
Cubist Head. 1937
(Tête cubiste)
Pencil, India ink and collage on cream paper,
9⅞ x 6½″ (25.1 x 16.4 cm.)
Signed and dated l.r.: *j.G. / 1937 / 12–4*
Collection Hans Hartung, Antibes

REFERENCE:
Gibert, vol. VIII, p. 101, repr.

180
Strange Head. 1937
(Tête étrange)
Colored pencil and India ink on mauve paper,
9⅞ x 9″ (25 x 23 cm.)
Signed and dated l.r.: *j.G.* / *1937* / *15–5*
Collection Museo Español de Arte Contemporáneo,
Madrid (Donación Roberta González)

REFERENCES:
Madrid, p. 172 (D-419)
Gibert, vol. VIII, p. 60, repr.

181
Reclining Figure. ca. 1936
(Personnage allongeé)
Pencil, ink and oil pastel on paper, 7½ x 10⅜″
(19.2 x 26.3 cm.)
Not signed or dated
Courtesy Galerie Beyeler, Basel

182
Reclining Figure. 1936
(Personnage étendu)
Colored pencil and India ink on paper mounted on
blue-gray paper, 9⅞ x 12⅞″ (25 x 32.6 cm.)
Not signed or dated
The Arthur and Madeleine Lejwa Collection,
New York
REFERENCE:
Gibert, vol. IX, p. 25, repr.

183
Reclining Figure. 1936
(Personnage couché)
India ink and wax crayon on paper, 8⅝ x 11⅛″
(22 x 29.5 cm.)
Signed and dated l.l.: *j.G. / 1936*
Collection Fondation Maeght, Saint-Paul-de-Vence,
France
REFERENCES:
Maeght, p. 31, no. 41
Gibert, vol. IX, p. 22, repr.

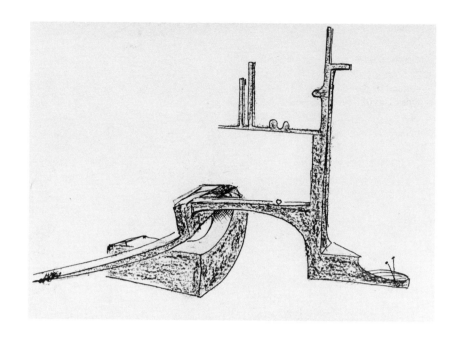

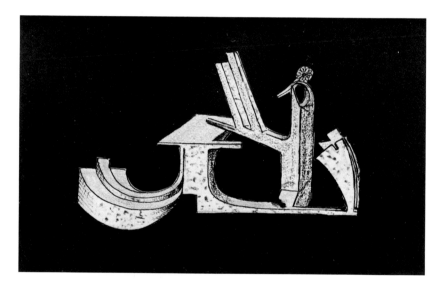

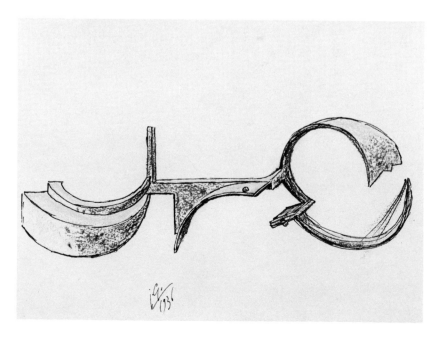

184
Reclining Figure. 1936
(Personnage allongé)
Bronze, 9⅞ x 15⅜ x 7½″ (25 x 39 x 19 cm.)
Not signed or dated
Courtesy David Grob, London

REFERENCE:
Withers, p. 82, fig. 96, p. 166, no. 109

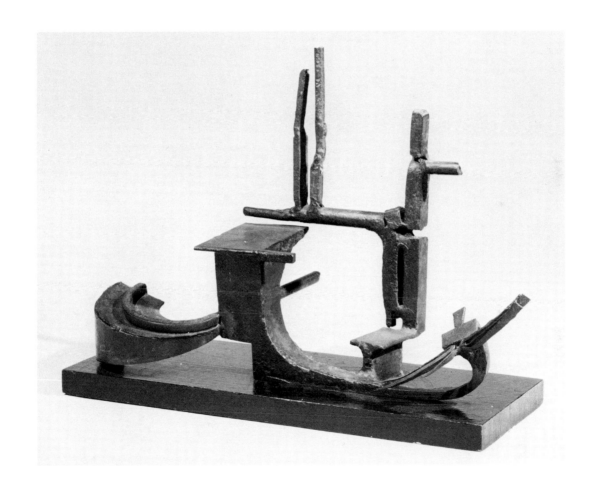

185
Reclining Figure. 1937
(Personnage allongé)
India ink, wax crayon and collage on paper,
6⅜ x 9⅞″ (16.3 x 25 cm.)
Signed and dated l.r.: *j.G. / 1937 / 20–3*
The Arthur and Madeleine Lejwa Collection,
New York

REFERENCE:
Gibert, vol. IX, p. 51, repr.

186
"Horizontal and Vertical" Figure. 1936
(Personnage dit "horizontal et vertical")
India ink and wax crayon on paper, irregular, ca.
7⅞ x 3¼″ (20 x 8 cm.)
Signed and dated l.l.: *j. G. / 1936*
Collection Dr. W. A. Bechtler, Zollikon

187
Reclining Figure. 1936
(Personnage étendu)
Colored pencil and India ink on paper, 6¼ x 9½″
(15.7 x 24 cm.)
Signed and dated l.l.: *j.G. / 1936*; inscribed l.r.:
*à L. Fernandez / en temoignage d' / une cordiale
amitié / j. Gonzalez / 1936*
Collection Museo de Arte Moderno, Barcelona, Gift
of Roberta González, 1972

REFERENCES:
Barcelona, p. 25, no. 107 (MAB 113.461)
Gibert, vol. IX, p. 24, repr.

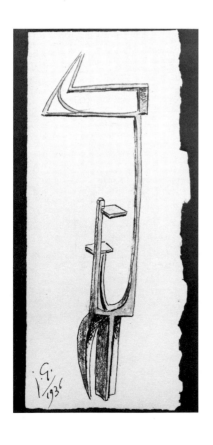

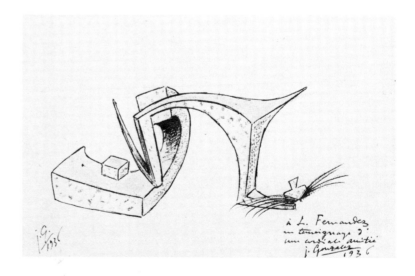

188
Reclining Figure. ca. 1936
(Personnage allongé)
Iron, 18 x 37 x 16¾″ (45.7 x 94 x 42.5 cm.)
Not signed or dated
Collection The Museum of Modern Art, New York,
Nelson A. Rockefeller Bequest, 1979
REFERENCE:
Withers, p. 82, fig. 94, p. 166, no. 107

189
Figure with a Mirror. 1936
(Personnage au miroir)
Colored pencil, India ink and watercolor on paper,
8⅞ x 8¼″ (22.5 x 21 cm.)
Signed and dated l.r.: *j.G. / 1936 / 16–9*
Collection Fondation Maeght, Saint-Paul-de-Vence,
France

REFERENCES:
Maeght, p. 31, no. 43
Gibert, vol. V, p. 59, repr.

190a
Seated Woman Combing Her Hair. 1936
(Femme assise se coiffant)
India ink and wax crayon on paper mounted on
paper, 11 x 7¼″ (28 x 18.6 cm.)
Signed and dated l.r.: *j.G. / 1936*
Collection Paul Haim, Paris

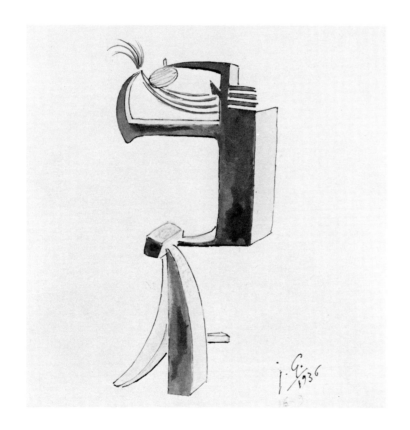

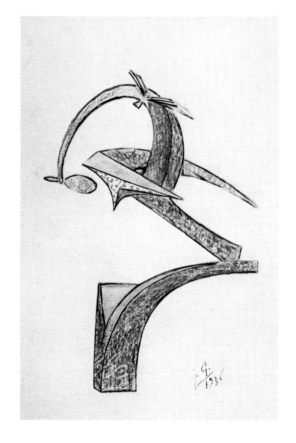

190b
Woman with a Mirror. 1936
(Femme au miroir)
India ink and wax crayon on paper mounted on
paper, 11 x 7¼″ (28 x 18.6 cm.)
Signed and dated l.l.: *j.G. / 1936*
Collection Paul Haim, Paris

REFERENCES:
Gibert, vol. V, pp. 57, 56, reprs.

191
Seated Woman Combing Her Hair. 1936
(Femme assise se coiffant)
India ink and oil pastel on paper, 9½ x 6⅜″
(24 x 16 cm.)
Signed and dated l.l.: *j.G. / 1936*
Courtesy Galerie de France, Paris

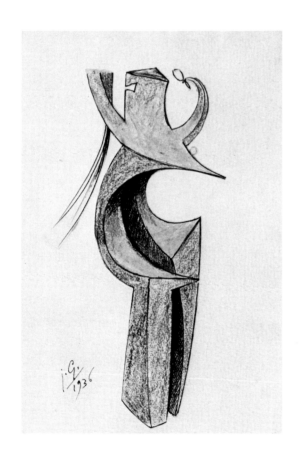

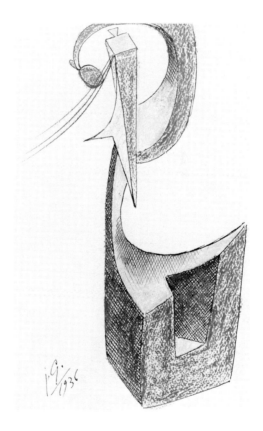

192
Study for "Woman Combing Her Hair." ca. 1936
(Etude pour "Femme se coiffant")
Pencil, crayon and India ink on paper, 8¼ x 5¾"
(20.8 x 14.4 cm.)
Not signed or dated; inscribed l.r.: *6*
Collection The Museum of Modern Art, New York,
Gift of Mme Roberta González-Richard

REFERENCE:
Gibert, vol. V, p. 59, repr.

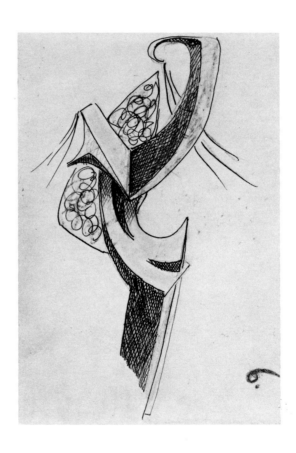

193
Woman Combing Her Hair. ca. 1936
(Femme se coiffant)
Iron, 52 x 23½ x 24⅝″ (132 x 59.7 x 62.6 cm.)
Not signed or dated
Collection The Museum of Modern Art, New York,
Mrs. Simon Guggenheim Fund, 1953

REFERENCE:
Withers, p. 81, fig. 92, p. 166, no. 108

194
Small Venus. ca. 1936
(Petite Vénus)
Iron, 8¼ x 2⅜ x 3¾″ (20.5 x 6 x 9.5 cm.)
Not signed or dated
Collection Carmen Martinez and Viviane
Grimminger, Paris
REFERENCE:
Withers, p. 85, fig. 104, p. 167, no. 112

We know almost nothing about González's relationship to Rodin. However, Rodin's reputation in Paris during the early decades of this century was so overwhelming that no one interested in sculpture could have remained unaware of him. Furthermore, González saved a newspaper announcing Rodin's death, which carried a full front page of illustrations of his sculptures (*Excelsior*, vol. 18, November 18, 1917). This seems to indicate that Rodin had personal significance for González.

González's private papers also contain reproductions of sculptures by Rodin, cut from a catalogue for an auction of 1914 (Collection of Anthony Roux, Galerie Georges Petit, Paris, May 19 and 20, 1914). These included an illustration of *Iris Awakening a Nymph* (fig.), a sculpture that at first glance evokes a Venus and Cupid subject. It is tempting to suggest that this was González's reading of the motif and that it may have inspired his *Small Venus*, which suggests the presence of a perched, winged figure.

Rodin's *Iris Awakening a Nymph* as reproduced in 1914 auction catalogue

195
Large Venus. ca. 1936
(Grande Vénus)
Iron, 12¼ x 4¼ x 3″ (31.1 x 10.8 x 7.6 cm.)
Not signed or dated
Collection Carmen Martinez and Viviane
Grimminger, Paris

REFERENCE:
Withers, p. 85, fig. 103, pp. 166-167, no. 111

196a
Peasant Woman from the Back. 1935
(Paysanne de dos)
Pencil and India ink on paper, 9½ x 6¼″
(24 x 16 cm.)
Signed and dated l.r.: *j. G. / 1935*
Collection Carmen Martinez and Viviane
Grimminger, Paris

196b
Peasant Woman with a Basket. ca. 1936
(Paysanne au panier)
Pencil, India ink and oil pastel on paper, 11 x 7½″
(28 x 19 cm.)
Not signed or dated
Collection Carmen Martinez and Viviane
Grimminger, Paris

REFERENCES:
Gibert, vol. II, pp. 217, 205, reprs.

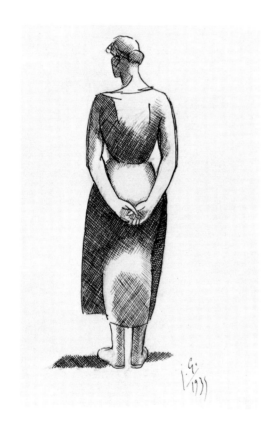

197
Large Silhouette of a Peasant Woman. ca. 1935
(Grand profil de paysanne)
Iron, 16⅞ x 5¾ x 2¾″ (42.8 x 14.5 x 7 cm.)
Not signed or dated
Collection Carmen Martinez and Viviane
Grimminger, Paris

REFERENCE:
Withers, p. 86, fig. 108, p. 164, no. 87

198
Large Female Torso. ca. 1935
(Grand buste féminin)
Iron, 21 x 10⅝ x 5¼″ (53.2 x 25.4 x 13.4 cm.)
Not signed or dated
Courtesy Carmen Martinez and Viviane
Grimminger, Paris

REFERENCE:
Withers, p. 166, no. 103

199

Woman with Infant. ca. 1929
(Femme au nourrisson)
Pencil, India ink and watercolor on paper,
6⅞ x 5¾" (17.5 x 14.6 cm.)
Signed and dated l.l.: *j. G. / 1929*
Collection Carmen Martinez and Viviane
Grimminger, Paris

REFERENCE:
Gibert, vol. III, p. 49, repr.

200

Mother and Child. 1936
(Maternité)
India ink, wash and watercolor on paper, 9½ x6"
(24 x 15.2 cm.)
Signed and dated l.r.: *j. G. / 1936*
Courtesy Galerie Beyeler, Basel

REFERENCE:
Gibert, vol. III, p. 76, repr.

In a letter of April 10, 1937, the Spanish Republican government invited González to contribute a sculpture to the Spanish pavilion at the 1937 *Exposition internationale des arts et techniques*. The exhibition opened in Paris on July 12, 1937, and included works by González, Miró and the sculptor Alberto as well as a fountain by Calder. González's *The Montserrat* was placed outside the pavilion designed by José Luis Sert and Luis Lacasa, to the right of the main entrance.

It seems probable that González had begun this sculpture as a simple motif of a peasant woman and child prior to receiving the formal invitation to exhibit; subsequently it would become a symbolic, patriotic statement. He had worked on Catalan peasant and maternity themes throughout his lifetime; he was a member of Spanish Republican circles in Paris; his concern for his countrymen was authentic and profound.

The title of this figure, one of the largest of González's career, refers to the mountain range visible from Barcelona that presents a saw-toothed profile (*serra* signifies *saw* in Catalan) and is the symbol of Catalonia. Apparently González was unsure whether to present this sculpture or a more abstract one, but he was persuaded by the exhibition's organizers that *The Montserrat* was the appropriate choice. (Pierre Descargues, *Julio Gonzalez*, Paris, 1971, p. 154)

201
The Montserrat. 1936-37
(La Montserrat)
Iron, 64¼ x 18½ x 18½" (165 x 47 x 47 cm.)
Not signed or dated
Collection Stedelijk Museum, Amsterdam

REFERENCE:
Withers, p. 90, fig. 115, p. 167, no. 118

202

"Sword" Figure. ca. 1937

(Personnage épée)

Pencil, ink and wax crayon on gray paper,
14½ x 8¾″ (36.9 x 22.2 cm.)

Not signed or dated

Courtesy The Pace Gallery, New York

REFERENCE:

Gibert, vol. IX, p. 38, repr.

203

Woman with Inclined Head. 1937

(Femme tête penchée)

India ink and oil pastel on yellow paper, 9⅞ x 6⅜″
(25.1 x 16.2 cm.)

Signed and dated l.l.: *j.G. / 1937 / 7–1*

Courtesy Galerie de France, Paris

REFERENCE:

Gibert, vol. IX, p. 39, repr.

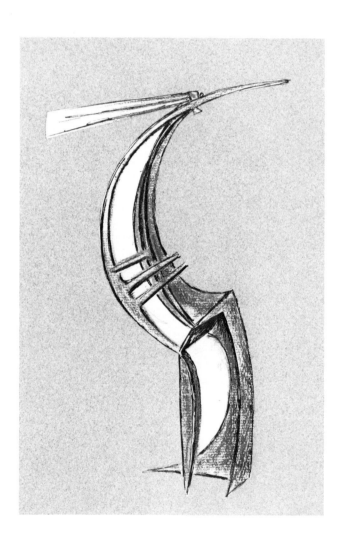

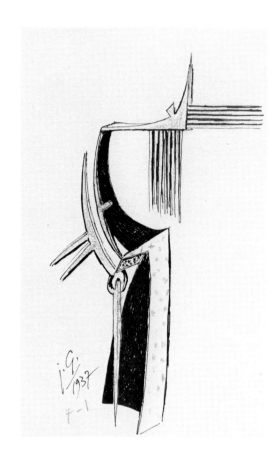

204
Small Sickle (Figure of a Woman). ca. 1937
(Petite faucille)
Forged bronze, 11¾ x 4½ x 3⅛″ (30 x 11.4 x 8 cm.)
Not signed or dated
Collection Adele and Irving Moscovitz, New York

REFERENCE:
Withers, p. 83, fig. 98, p. 167, no. 114

205
Figure with Sickle. 1937
(Personnage à la faucille)
India ink and collage on siena paper, 12¾ x 9⅞″
(32.5 x 25 cm.)
Signed and dated l.l.: *j. G. / 1937 / 23–3*
Collection The Solomon R. Guggenheim Museum,
New York, Gift of Carmen Martinez and Viviane
Grimminger

REFERENCE:
Gibert, vol. IX, p. 53, repr.

206
Large Sickle. ca. 1937
(Grande faucille)
Forged bronze, 17⅞ x 4¾ x 1⅝″ (45.5 x 12 x 4 cm.)
Not signed or dated
Courtesy Galerie de France, Paris

REFERENCE:
Withers, p. 83, fig. 97, p. 167, no. 113

207
Gothic Man. 1937
(L'Homme gothique)
Iron, 19¾ x 10½ x 5 ⅛″ (50 x 26.5 x 13 cm.)
Signed and dated on stone base: *j. Gonzalez*
Collection Hans Hartung, Antibes

REFERENCE:
Withers, p. 95, fig. 124, p. 167, no. 120

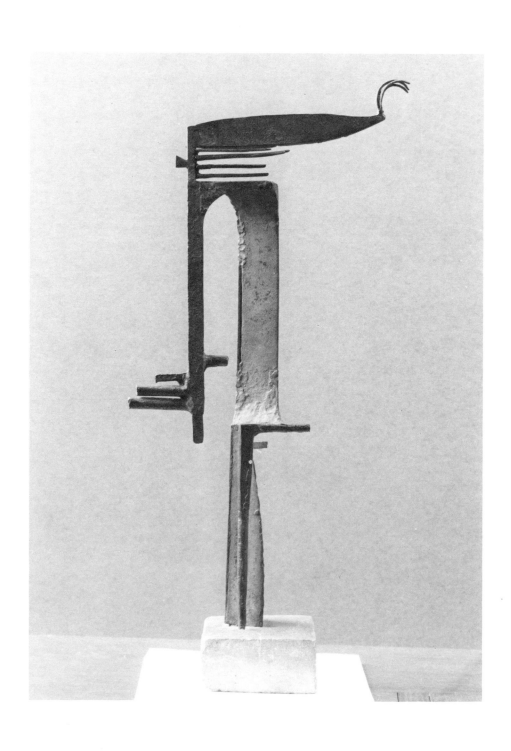

208
Figure with White Square. 1937
(Personnage au carré blanc)
India ink, pastel and collage on beige paper,
13 x 10″ (33 x 25.5 cm.)
Signed and dated l.l.: *j. G. / 1937 / 16–3*
Courtesy Galerie de France, Paris

REFERENCE:
Gibert, vol. IX, p. 50, repr.

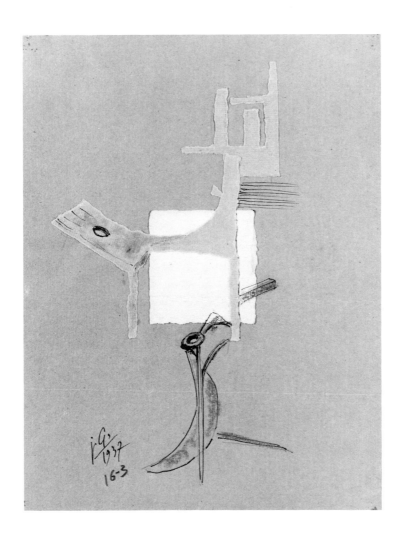

209

Study for "Woman with a Mirror." 1937
(Etude pour "Femme au miroir")
Black and colored pencils, ink and oil pastel on
red-brown paper, 13⅜ x 9⅝″ (34 x 24.5 cm.)
Signed and dated l.r.: *j. G. / 1937 / 14–7*
Collection Carmen Martinez and Viviane
Grimminger, Paris

REFERENCE:
Gibert, vol. V, p. 68, repr.

210

Study for "Woman with a Mirror." 1937
(Etude pour "Femme au miroir")
India ink and oil pastel on paper, 15 x 11″
(38.2 x 28.1 cm.)
Signed and dated l.l.: *j. G. / 1937 7–8*
Collection Hans Hartung, Antibes

REFERENCE:
Gibert, vol. IX, p. 55, repr.

211

Woman with a Mirror. ca. 1937
(Femme au miroir)
Iron, 80¼ x 30 x 16⅝″ (203.8 x 76 x 42 cm.)
Not signed or dated
Collection Carmen Martinez and Viviane
Grimminger, Paris

REFERENCE:
Withers, p. 88, fig. 109, p. 167, no. 117

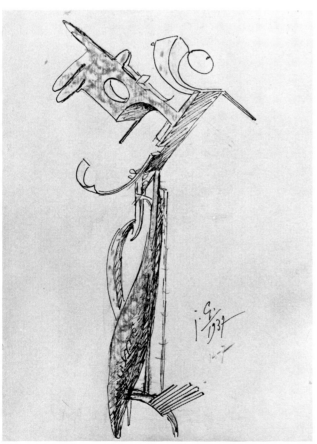

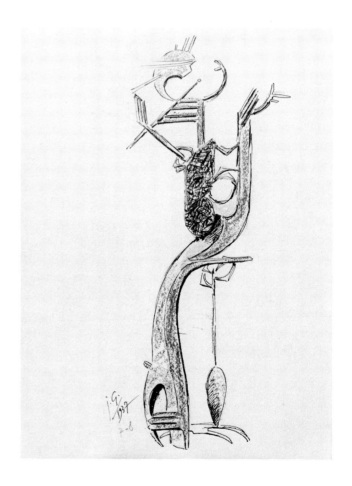

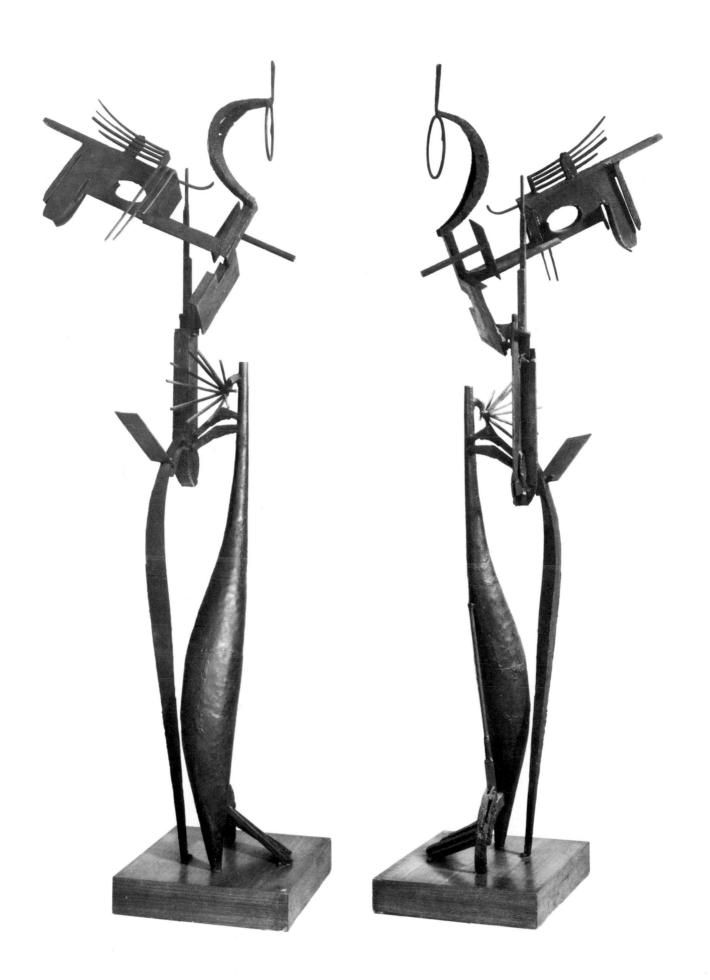

175

212
Dancer Holding a Daisy. ca. 1937
(Danseuse à la marguerite)
Iron, 19 x 11½ x 4″ (48.3 x 29.2 x 10 cm.)
Not signed or dated
Collection Carmen Martinez and Viviane
Grimminger, Paris

REFERENCE:
Withers, p. 84, fig. 100, p. 167, no. 116

213
"Daisy" Figure with Large Hands. 1938
(Personnage marguerite aux grandes mains)
Colored pencil and India ink on paper, 12⅝ x 9½″
(32 x 24 cm.)
Signed and dated l.r.: *12-11-38 | j.G.*
Collection Fondation Maeght, Saint-Paul-de-Vence,
France

REFERENCES:
Maeght, p. 32, no. 49
Gibert, vol. IX, p. 76, repr.

214
Study for a Metal Sculpture. 1939
(Etude pour une sculpture)
Pencil, brown ink and wash on paper, 12¾ x 9⅞″
(32.5 x 25 cm.)
Signed and dated l.r.: *(Noël) | 25-12-39 | j.G.*
Collection Rijksmuseum Kröller-Müller, Otterlo,
Gift of Roberta González

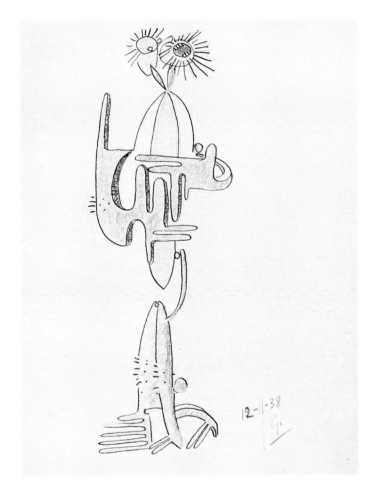

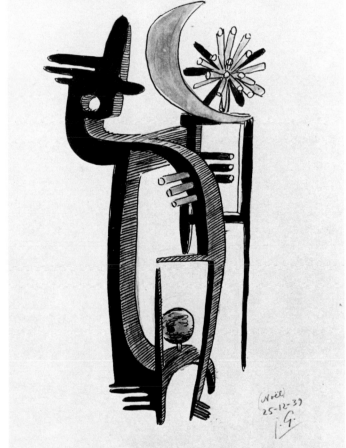

215a
Austere Form. ca. 1937
(Forme sévère)
Iron, 31⅛ x 8¾ x 11½″ (79.2 x 22.3 x 29.1 cm.)
Not signed or dated
Collection Hans Hartung, Antibes

215b
Slender Form. ca. 1937
(Forme très fine)
Iron, 34⅜ x 3 x 6⅝″ (87.3 x 7.7 x 16.8 cm.)
Not signed or dated
Collection Hans Hartung, Antibes

215c
Taut Form. ca. 1937
(Forme rigide)
Iron, 26½ x 12 x 10¼″ (67.2 x 30.7 x 26 cm.)
Not signed or dated
Collection Hans Hartung, Antibes

215d
Pair of Hands. ca. 1937
(Les Deux mains)
Iron, 28 x 10¼ x 14⅜″ (71 x 26 x 36.5 cm.)
Not signed or dated
Collection Hans Hartung, Antibes

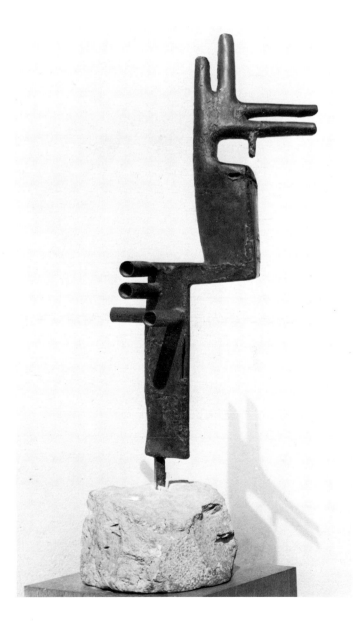

216
Screaming Head. 1938
(Tête criant)
Charcoal and oil pastel on paper, 11⅞ x 8″
(30.1 x 20.3 cm.)
Signed and dated l.r.: *30-11-38 / j.G.*
Collection Museo de Arte Moderno, Barcelona,
Gift of Roberta González, 1972

REFERENCES:
Barcelona, p. 26, no. 123 (MAB 113.542)
Gibert, vol. II, p. 332, repr.

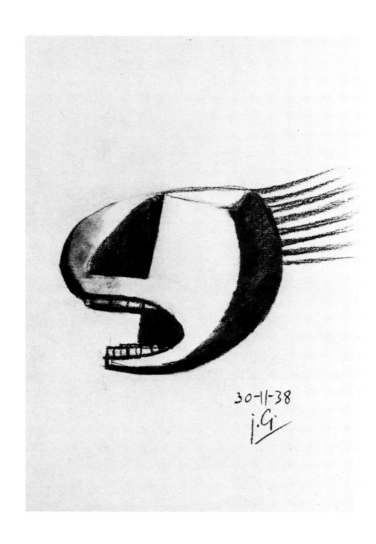

217
Study for "Monsieur Cactus" (Cactus Man). 1938
(Etude pour "L'Homme Cactus")
India ink, wash and wax crayon on paper,
11¾ x 6¼″ (30 x 16 cm.)
Signed and dated l.r.: *3-12-38 | j. G.*
Private Collection

REFERENCE:
Gibert, vol. IX, p. 81, repr.

218
Rectangular Figure. 1938
(Personnage rectangulaire)
Pencil, India ink, wax crayon and chalk on paper,
9⅞ x 6⅞″ (25 x 17.4 cm.)
Signed and dated l.r.: *5-12-38 | j.G.*
The Arthur and Madeleine Lejwa Collection,
New York

REFERENCE:
Gibert, vol. IX, p. 80, repr.

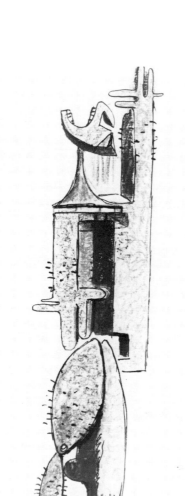

219
Study for "Monsieur Cactus" (Cactus Man). 1939
(Etude pour "L'Homme cactus")
India ink and oil pastel on paper, 12¾ x 9⅞"
(32.4 x 25 cm.)
Signed and dated l.r.: *9-4-39 / j. G.*; inscribed l.c.:
dos
Collection Hans Hartung, Antibes
REFERENCE:
Gibert, vol. IX, p. 85, repr.

220
Study for "Monsieur Cactus" (Cactus Man). 1939
(Etude pour "L'Homme cactus")
India ink and oil pastel on beige paper, 8⅜ x 6⅜"
(21.2 x 16.2 cm.)
Signed and dated l.r.: *11-4-39 / j.G.*
Collection Hans Hartung, Antibes
REFERENCE:
Gibert, vol. IX, p. 92, repr.

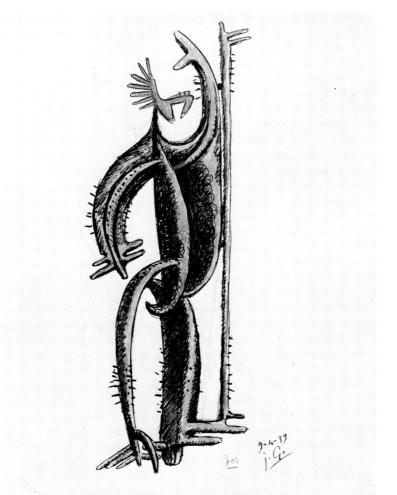

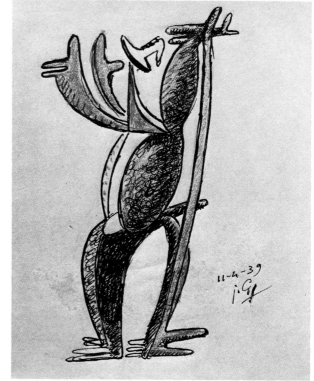

221
Study for "Monsieur Cactus" (Cactus Man). 1939
(Etude pour "L'Homme cactus")
Pencil, India ink and wax crayon on paper,
12¼ x 7⅞″ (31 x 20 cm.)
Signed and dated l.r.: *22-1-39 / j. G.*
Private Collection

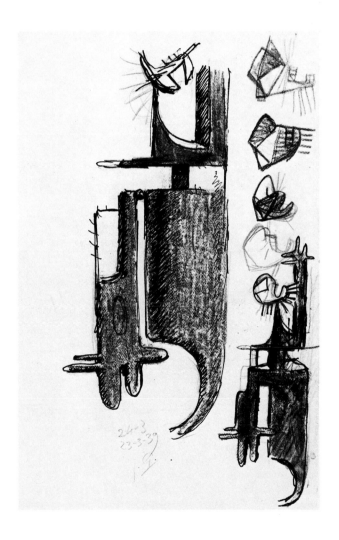

222

Head with Open Mouth. 1939
(Tête à la bouche ouverte)
Pencil and India ink on paper, 12¾ x 10⅛″
(32.5 x 25.7 cm.)
Signed and dated l.r.: *24-1-39 | j. G.*
Collection Musée National d'Art Moderne, Centre
Georges Pompidou, Paris, Don de Roberta Gonzalez

REFERENCE:
Gibert, vol. II, p. 337, repr.

223

Head Called "Teeth." 1939
(Tête "Les Dents")
Colored pencil and India ink on beige paper,
7½ x 11⅜″ (19 x 29 cm.)
Signed and dated l.r.: *22-1-39 | j. G.*
Private Collection

REFERENCE:
Gibert, vol. II, p. 336, repr.

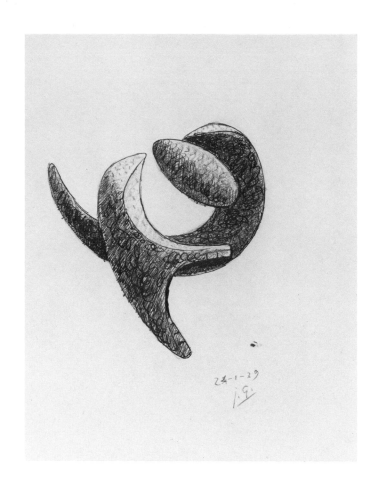

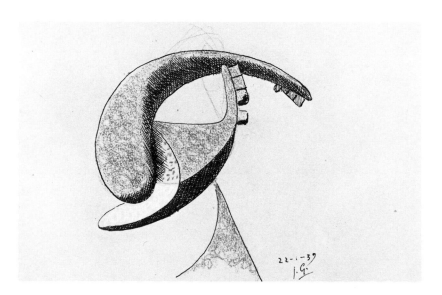

224
Dramatic Head. 1939
(Tête dramatique)
Colored pencil and India ink on paper, 9⅞ x 12¾"
(25 x 32.4 cm.)
Signed and dated l.l.: *31-1-39 / j. G.*
Private Collection

REFERENCE:
Gibert, vol. II, p. 343, repr.

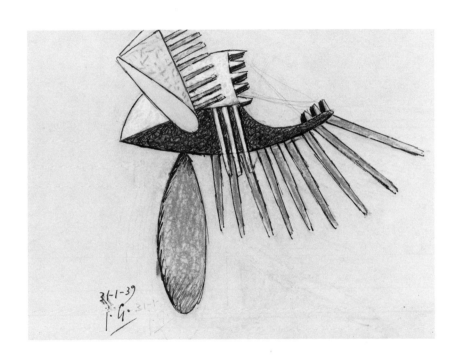

Constantin Brancusi
The First Cry. 1914
Bronze, 9⅞" (25.1 cm.) long
Collection Dr. W. A. Bechtler, Zollikon

Starting in 1929 González executed four "reclining" heads in metal: *Reclining Head*, 1929 (Private Collection, Paris); *Reclining Head Called "Spanish Mask,"* 1930 (cat. no. 80); *Small Silver Mask*, ca. 1934 (Collection Musée National d'Art Moderne, Centre Georges Pompidou, Paris); and *Cowled Head*, ca. 1939, as well as a number of renditions in plaster and stone. It may be suggested that the subject was inspired by González's frequenting of Brancusi's studio. Indeed, the singularly smooth surface and self-contained oval silhouette of *Cowled Head* recall Brancusi's subjects *The First Cry*, 1914 (Collection Dr. W. A. Bechtler, Zollikon) (fig.) and *The Newborn*, 1915 (Collection The Museum of Modern Art, New York), even though its proportions are extremely different.

There is speculation (conversation with Jörn Merkert, December 1981) that González was referring in this piece to a Spanish terrorist group that emerged during the Civil War and was known in France as *Les Cagoulards*, because of the hoods and masks worn by its members.

225
Cowled Head. ca. 1939
(Le Cagoulard)
Forged bronze, 5⅞ x 9½ x 7⅞″ (15 x 24 x 20 cm.)
Not signed or dated
Collection Carmen Martinez and Viviane
Grimminger, Paris

reference:
Withers, p. 80, fig. 88, p. 164, no. 90

226
Monsieur Cactus (Cactus Man I) 1939
(L'Homme cactus I)
Iron, 26¼ x 9⅞ x 5⅛″ (66.5 x 25 x 13 cm.)
Not signed or dated
Collection Carmen Martinez and Viviane
Grimminger, Paris

REFERENCE:
Withers, p. 88, fig. 110, p. 168, no. 121

Although this work is traditionally known as *Cactus Man I* and variously dated between 1938 and 1940, two postcards and a letter from González to his daughter Roberta indicate another title and the exact date of its completion. All three documents refer to the sculpture as *"Monsieur Cactus."* The final letter, dated August 24, 1939, states: *"Monsieur Cactus est terminé (C'est une bonne nouvelle)."* (Monsieur Cactus is finished. Good news.)

That this sculpture depicts a masculine figure is clear from its squared, rather heavy silhouette, the mustache, beard and hairy limbs, not to mention the prominent phallus. An examination of the 1938-39 drawings confirms this interpretation. The drawings also suggest analogies with Pablo Gargallo's sculpture of 1934, *The Prophet* (fig.), which González surely knew either from the artist's studio or from its annual exhibition in the years 1937 to 1939 in Paris.

Study for "Monsieur Cactus" (Cactus Man) (cat. no. 219) shows the same singular curves in the central torso seen in Gargallo's sculpture. It also shows analogies in the dissected structure composed of separate muscles, tendons or skeletal axes conjoined (compare, for example, the legs of *The Prophet* to the arms in González's drawing). Many of the drawings suggest rounded open areas within the anatomy like those in Gargallo's sculpture. However, the most striking analogy is in each figure's stance and accessory stave. Although the image of *The Prophet* may have contributed to González's inspiration, as he began to interpret it in his own terms, his forms and articulations became more abstract and personal. In the final sculpture little reminiscence of Gargallo's piece remains apparent. The iconography and the syntax are González's own, derived from a welding rather than a casting process.

Pablo Gargallo
The Prophet. 1933
Bronze, 92¾" (235 cm.) high
Collection Musée National d'Art Moderne, Centre Georges Pompidou, Paris

227
Seated Woman. 1938-39
(Femme assise)
Ink and wash on beige paper, 9½ x 12¼″
(24 x 31 cm.)
Signed and dated l.r.: *5-2-38/39 | j.G.*
Collection Michael and Juliet Rubenstein, New York

REFERENCE:
Gibert, vol. IX, p. 65, repr.

228
Strange Woman. 1939
(Femme étrange)
India ink on paper, 12¼ x 7⅞″ (31 x 20 cm.)
Signed and dated l.r.: *16 / 17-2-39 / j.G.*
Courtesy Galerie de France, Paris

REFERENCE:
Gibert, vol. IX, p. 98, repr.

229
Long Hair. 1939
(La Longue chevelure)
Pencil, India ink and wash on pink paper, 11 x 5¾″
(28 x 14.5 cm.)
Signed and dated l.r.: *4-5-39 / j.G.*
Collection Museo Español de Arte Contemporáneo,
Madrid (Donación Roberta González)

REFERENCES:
Madrid, p. 173 (D-405)
Gibert, vol. IX, p. 93, repr.

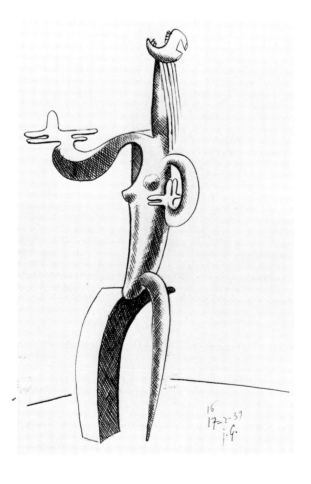

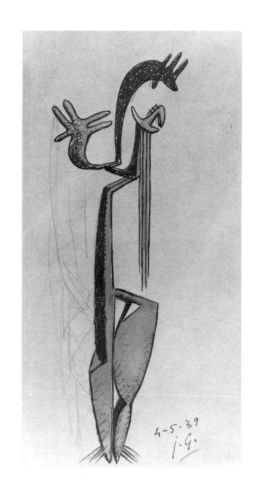

233
Madame Cactus (Cactus Man II). 1939-40
(L'Homme Cactus II)
Bronze, 30¾" (78 cm.) high
Posthumous cast from iron original
Inscribed l. side of rear leg: ⅔ / (*X/DV/R.
Gonzalez*)
Collection Museum of Fine Arts, Houston, Museum
Purchase

REFERENCE:
Withers, p. 88, fig. 111, p. 168, no. 122

Unlike *Monsieur Cactus* (cat. no. 226), this sculpture seems to represent a female silhouette, an impression transmitted by the more delicate limbs and articulations and the fluid arabesque of the whole configuration. Many drawings of 1939-40, depicting a female cactus figure with flowing hair, enable us to read this image in these terms and suggest its logical identification as a "Madame Cactus."[1]

A further reference may be found in Jules Lefebvre's painting of *Truth* (fig.), which had been in the collection of the Musée du Luxembourg in Paris since 1874, and was published in that museum's collection catalogue of 1892 and widely reproduced. (It was subsequently transferred to Amiens.) González would have been sensitive to Lefebvre's allegory of truth; and Lefebvre's subject is a woman with a mirror, one of González's favored themes (see cat nos. 137, 144, 210). Moreover, analogies between the formal conception of the painting and the sculpture are striking.

The original version of *Madame Cactus* (Collection Staatliche Kunsthalle, Karlsruhe, West Germany) was not available for the present exhibition. Because of the importance of this sculpture in González's oeuvre, a posthumous bronze cast is included here.

Jules Lefebvre
Truth. 1870
Oil on canvas, 103⅛ x 43⅜" (262 x 110 cm.)
Collection Musée de Picardie, Amiens

1. This author disagrees with E. A. Carmean in his formal reading and interpretation of this sculpture as stated in his essay "Cactus Man Number Two," in *The Bulletin of the Museum of Fine Arts, Houston*, vol. IV, no. 3, Fall 1973, pp. 38-45.

238
Screaming Montserrat. 1940
(Montserrat criant)
Pencil and India ink on paper, 9½ x 12½"
(24 x 31.6 cm.)
Signed and dated c.r.: *2-6-40 / j. G.*
Courtesy Galerie Beyeler, Basel

REFERENCE:
Gibert, vol. II, p. 226, repr.

239
Screaming Montserrat. 1941
(Montserrat criant)
Pencil and India ink on paper, 9⅞ x 10"
(25 x 25.4 cm.)
Dated l.l.: *18-11-41* Not signed
Collection Carmen Martinez and Viviane
Grimminger, Paris

REFERENCE:
Gibert, vol. II, p. 275, repr.

240

Mask of the Screaming Montserrat. ca. 1941-42
(Masque de la Montserrat criant)
Iron, 9⅛ x 6⅛ x 4¾″ (23 x 15.5 x 12 cm.)
Not signed or dated
Collection Musée National d'Art Moderne, Centre
Georges Pompidou, Paris, Don de Mme R. Gonzalez
REFERENCE:
Withers, p. 92, fig. 119, p. 167, no. 119

243a
Raised Right Hand (No. 1). ca. 1942
(Main droite levée [no. 1])
Bronze, 16⅝″ (42 cm.) high
Posthumous cast from plaster original
Inscribed bottom: *a.B. Fond. d'Art Paris / Gonzalez*
© *3/8*
Courtesy Galerie de France, Paris

243b
Raised Left Hand (No. 2). ca. 1942
(Main gauche levée [no. 2])
Bronze, 14¼″ (36 cm.) high
Posthumous cast from plaster original
Inscribed bottom: *Gonzalez* © *3/8*
Courtesy Galerie de France, Paris

One of González's late ambitions was to make a large version of the *Small Frightened Montserrat* (cat. no. 241). As was his practice, and common practice at the time, he began by executing parts of the sculpture separately with the intention of mounting them together subsequently. The *Raised Right Hand, Raised Left Hand* and the *Head of the Screaming Montserrat* (cat. nos. 243, 242) were the first pieces undertaken for this projected sculpture, which, unfortunately, was not realized because of the artist's death in 1942. Compare the positions of these hands to those in the two drawings of the *Screaming Montserrat* (cat. nos. 238, 239).

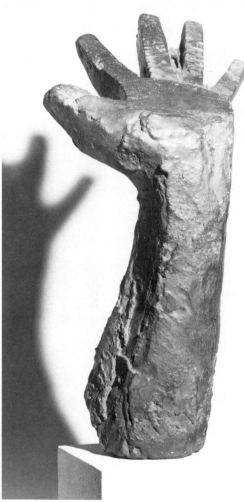

244
Cactus Man with Book. 1941
(L'Homme cactus au livre)
India ink and wash on paper, 12⅝ x 10″
(32 x 25.5 cm.)
Dated l.r.: *3-1-41* Not signed
Collection Fondation Maeght, Saint-Paul-de-Vence,
France

REFERENCES:
Maeght, p. 32, no. 51
Gibert, vol. IX, p. 121, repr.

245
Large Figure. 1941
(Grand personnage)
Black pastel on paper, 28¾ x 20⅞″ (73 x 53 cm.)
Signed and dated l.l.: *29-1-41 / j.G.*
Collection Fondation Maeght, Saint-Paul-de-Vence,
France

REFERENCES:
Maeght, p. 15, repr., p. 32, no. 53
Gibert, vol. IX, p. 173, repr.

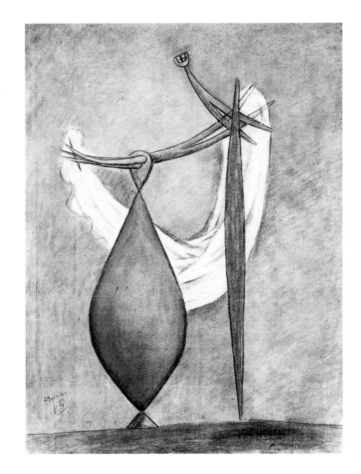

246
Figure. 1941
(Personnage)
India ink and watercolor on beige paper, 11⅛ x 7⅜″
(28.3 x 18.7 cm.)
Signed and dated l.r.: *22-1-41 / j. G.*
Collection Hans Hartung, Antibes

<small>REFERENCE:</small>
Gibert, vol. IX, p. 113, repr.

247
Extraordinary Figure. ca. 1941
(Personnage extraordinaire)
India ink, gouache and oil pastel on paper,
14⅝ x 10¼″ (37.3 x 26 cm.)
Not signed or dated
Collection Carmen Martinez and Viviane
Grimminger, Paris

REFERENCE:
Gibert, vol. IX, p. 133, repr.

EXHIBITIONS

ELIZABETH A. BROWN

1922
Paris, Galerie Povolovsky, *Julio Gonzalez*, March 1-15. Invitation with text by Alexandre Mercereau, reprinted from *Les Hommes du jour*, October 1920. Sculptures, works on paper, paintings, jewelry, decorative objects

1923
Paris, Galerie du Caméléon [González], January 1-15. Organized by Alexandre Mercereau.
Sculptures, works on paper, paintings, enamels, jewelry, decorative objects

1930
Paris, Galerie de France [González], February. Catalogue with text by Louis Vauxcelles.
Iron sculptures

1931
Brussels, Galerie Le Centaure, *J. Gonzalez: sculptures présentées par la Galerie de France*, May 30-June 10. Catalogue with text by Lucien Farnoux-Renaud.
17 sculptures

1934
Paris, Galerie Percier, *J. Gonzalez*, April 25-May 8. Catalogue with text by Maurice Raynal.
Sculptures, watercolors

1935
Paris, Galerie des Cahiers d'Art, *Julio Gonzalez: Sculptures*, November 20-30. Organized by Yvonne Zervos.
Iron sculptures

1937
Paris, Galerie Pierre, *Sculptures et dessins de Gonzalez*, May 12-26.
Sculptures, drawings

1952
Paris, Musée National d'Art Moderne, *Julio Gonzalez: Sculptures*, February 1-March 9. Catalogue with text by Jean Cassou.
115 sculptures; enamels, drawings

1954
Munich, Galerie Otto Stangl, *Julio Gonazlez 1876-1942: Plastiken und Zeichnungen*, August 20-September. Included paintings by Roberta González.
Ca. 12 sculptures, 20 drawings

Cologne, Galerie der Spiegel, *Julio Gonzalez—Plastik und Zeichnungen*, October 13-November 10.
10 sculptures, 15 drawings

1955
Amsterdam, Stedelijk Museum, *Julio Gonzalez*, April 7-May 10. Catalogue with text by P.-G. Bruguière, reprinted from *Cahiers d'Art*, XXVIIᵉ année, July 1952, pp. 19-26.

119 sculptures, 59 drawings, 3 paintings, 6 enamels
Traveled to Brussels, Palais des Beaux-Arts, May 20-June 19; Kunsthalle Bern, July 2-August 7, separate catalogue with text by A. Rüdlinger; La Chaux-de-fonds, Switzerland, Musée des Beaux-Arts, August 26-September 25, separate catalogue with text by P. Seylaz.

1956
New York, The Museum of Modern Art, *Julio Gonzalez*, February 7-April 8. *Museum of Modern Art Bulletin*, vol. XXIII, nos. 1-2, 1955-56, text by Andrew C. Ritchie, reprinted text by González, as catalogue.
57 sculptures, 35 drawings
Traveled to Minneapolis Institute of Arts, May 8-June 17.

New York, Kleeman Gallery, *Julio Gonzalez*, March 12-April 7. Catalogue with text by Charlotte Weidler.
12 sculptures, 37 drawings

1957
Paris, Galerie Berggruen et Cie., *Julio Gonzalez: Dessins et aquarelles*, April. Catalogue with text by Georges A. Salles.
Ca. 50 works on paper
Hannover, Kestner-Gesellschaft, *Julio Gonzalez*, November 1-December 1. Catalogue with text by Werner Schmalenbach.
75 sculptures, 2 paintings, 2 enamels; works on paper
Traveled to Krefeld, Museum Haus Lange, December 15, 1957-March 2, 1958; Dortmund, Museum am Ostwall, April; Städtisches Museum Leverkusen, Schloss Morsbroich, May.

1959
Paris, Galerie de France, *Julio Gonzalez*, January 16-February. Catalogue with text by Roberta González, reprinted text by González; excerpts from earlier catalogues and reviews.
16 sculptures

1960
Sala de Santa Catalina del Ateneo de Madrid, *Julio González*, March 17-April 18. Catalogue with texts by Padre Alfonso Roig, González and Roberta González.
37 sculptures, 7 drawings
Traveled to Barcelona, Palacio de la Virreina, April 27-May 27.

1961
New York, Galerie Chalette, *Julio Gonzalez*, October 16-November 28. Catalogue with text by Hilton Kramer.
57 sculptures, 41 works on paper, 5 enamels
Traveled to San Francisco Museum of Art, February 1-March 4, 1962; Cleveland Museum of Art,

July 12-August 5; Utica, Munson-Williams-Proctor Institute, December 9, 1962-February 10, 1963; Buffalo, Albright-Knox Art Gallery, May 15-June 12; Montreal Museum of Fine Arts, August 21-September 23; Ottawa, National Gallery of Canada, October.

1963
Stockholm, Galerie Samlaren [González], December 7, 1963-January 4, 1964. Catalogue.
22 sculptures, 30 drawings, 4 rings

1964
French Pavilion, *XXXIIe Biennale de Venezia: Julio González*, June 20-October 18. Catalogue with text by Jean Cassou; special issue of *Papeles de Son Armadans*, Madrid, no. CVII, February 1965, text by Vicente Aguilera Cerni, as additional catalogue.
35 sculptures, 17 drawings

1965
Paris, Galerie de France, *Joan, Julio et Roberta Gonzalez: Peintures et dessins inédits*, April 9-May 30. Catalogue with text by Pierre Descargues.
18 works on paper, 10 paintings by Julio González

Los Angeles, Felix Landau Gallery, *Julio Gonzalez: Sculptures, Paintings, and Drawings*, October 4-30. Brochure.
30 sculptures, 64 drawings, 4 paintings

1967
Turin, Galleria Civica d'Arte Moderna, *Julio Gonzalez*, April-May. Catalogue with text by Luigi Malle, reprinted and translated texts by Vicente Aguilera Cerni, Pierre Descargues, Roberta González and Werner Schmalenbach.
9 sculptures, 98 works on paper, 7 paintings

1968
Madrid, Sala de Santa Catalina del Ateneo, *Joan González, Julio González, Roberta González*, March 22-May 10. *Publicaciones españolas, cuaderno de arte*, no. 247, edited by Carlos-Antonio Arean, with reprinted texts by Pierre Descargues, Charles Estienne, González, Maurice Raynal as catalogue.
Traveled to Barcelona, Palau de la Virreina, May 17-September 6.

San Juan, Puerto Rico, Instituto de Cultura Puertorriqueña, *Julio Gonzalez, Drawings and Sculptures*, November 15-December 8. Brochure with text by Josephine Withers.
5 sculptures, 52 drawings
Traveled to New York, The Museum of Modern Art (organizer), January 22, 1968-March 16, 1969; San Diego Museum of Art, April 18-May 11; Austin, University of Texas Art Museum, June 1-29; Arts Club of Chicago, September 22-October 19, with additional loans of 12 sculptures, 14 drawings; Ath-

ens, Georgia Museum of Art, University of Georgia, February 15-March 15, 1970; Gainesville, University of Florida Art Museum, April 5-27; Waltham, Massachusetts, Rose Art Gallery, Brandeis University, May 17-June 28; College Park, University of Maryland Art Gallery, September 17-October 11; Oberlin, Ohio, Allen Memorial Art Museum, Oberlin College, November 2-20; Edmonton, Canada, Edmonton Art Gallery, January 4-31, 1971

1969
New York, Saidenberg Gallery, *Julio Gonzalez: The Materials of his Expression*, March 14-May 1.
53 sculptures, 49 drawings
Traveled to Galerie de Montreal, September 17-October; Toronto, Dunkelman Gallery, November 8-22; Zürich, Gimpel et Hanover Galerie, as *Julio Gonzalez: Bronzen, Eisenplastiken, Zeichnungen*, January 14-February 21, 1970; Paris, Galerie de France (organizer), April 17-June 15. Catalogue with texts by Gildo Caputo, Roberta González, Hans Hartung, Myriam Prévot-Douatte and Josephine Withers; reprinted texts by Carlos-Antonio Arean, Jean Cassou, Hilton Kramer, M. N. Pradel, Andrew C. Ritchie, R. P. Alfonso Roig, Werner Schmalenbach and P. Seylaz; Essen, Museum Folkwang, July 5-August 16; London, Gimpel Fils, Ltd., September 9-October 15, drawings, and The Tate Gallery, September 15-October 15, sculptures, with additional loans; Montpellier, France, Musée Fabre, November 12, 1970-January 15, 1971; Høvikkoden, Norway, Sonja Henies og Niels Onstads Foundation, February 6-23; Cologne, Baukunst Galerie, March 18-May 8; Munich, Staatliche Graphische Sammlung, May 26-July 4; Edinburgh, Scottish National Gallery of Modern Art, August 14-September 12; Rome, Galleria Il Collezionista, October 14-December 31

1972
Gentofte, Denmark, Gentofte Rådhus, *Julio Gonzalez*, January 29-February 13.
82 sculptures, 31 drawings

Saint-Paul-de-Vence, France, Fondation Maeght, *Donation Gonzalez*, June 9-July 4. Catalogue with text by Jean-Louis Prat.
3 sculptures, 50 works on paper by Julio González

Madrid, Galeria Theo, *Julio González: Pinturas 1920-1937*, October 20-November 20. Catalogue with text by Julian Gállego.
23 paintings; drawings

1973
Barcelona, Sala Gaspar, *Homage a Julio González*, December 11, 1973-January 6, 1974. On occasion of publication of Vicente Aguilera Cerni, *Julio González*, Barcelona.
18 sculptures, 100 drawings

1974

Cologne, Galerie Dreiseitel, *Julio Gonzalez—Zeichnungen: 1928-1942*, March 8-April 30. Catalogue with text by Günter Metken, reprinted text by Vicente Aguilera Cerni.
35 drawings

Valencia, Galeria Punto, *Julio González*, March 8-April 10. Brochure.
18 sculptures, 70 drawings

Madrid, Galeria Turner [González], May.
Drawings, paintings

Barcelona, Museo de Arte Moderno, *Donación González*, June. Catalogue by Rosa M. Subirana and Eloisa Sendra, with text by J. Ainaud de Lasarte.
47 sculptures, 12 decorative objects, 2 enamels by Julio González.

Madrid, Galeria Ruíz Castillo, *Julio González*, October-November. Catalogue with text and reprinted text by Vicente Aguilera Cerni.
10 sculptures; drawings

1975

Tokyo, Contemporary Sculpture Center, *Exposition Julio Gonzalez au Japon*, October 1-18. Catalogue with texts in Japanese by Cécile Goldscheider, Roberta González, Myriam Prévot-Douatte, Alexandre Mercereau.
12 sculptures, 11 works on paper
Traveled to Osaka, Contemporary Sculpture Center, November 9-20.

Paris, Galerie de France, *Julio Gonzalez Sculptures*, November 19-December 31. On occasion of publication of Josette Gibert, *Julio Gonzalez dessins*, 9 vols., Paris.
10 sculptures, 15 works on paper

Paris, Galerie Carmen Martinez, *Julio Gonzalez Dessins*, November 20-December 31. On occasion of publication of Josette Gibert, *Julio Gonzalez dessins*, 9 vols., Paris.

1976

New York, The Pace Gallery, *Gonzalez: 100th Anniversary Exhibition*, March 27-April 24. Catalogue with text by David Smith, reprinted from *Art News*, vol. 54, February 1956, pp. 35-37 ff.
28 sculptures, 30 drawings
Traveled to Central Pavilion, *Biennale 76 di Venezia: Omaggio alla Spagna democratica*, June 13-October 10.

1977

Städtische Kunsthalle Mannheim, *Julio Gonzalez, 1876-1942: Plastik und Zeichnungen*, March 30-May 1. Catalogue with texts by Heinz Fuchs and Rudolf Oxenaar.

59 sculptures, 31 drawings
Traveled in part to Vienna, Galerie Ulysses, May 23-June 30; Salzburger Kunstverein, July 15-August 15.

Hannover, Galerie Brusberg, *Julio Gonzalez: Bronzen und Zeichnungen, eine Retrospektive*, September 11-October 22.
45 sculptures, 24 drawings

Charleroi, Belgium, Palais des Beaux-Arts, *Sculptures et dessins de Julio Gonzalez*, November 12-December 18. Catalogue with text by Robert Rousseau.
57 sculptures, 35 drawings

1978

Hamburg, Galerie Wentzel, *Julio Gonzalez: Skulpturen und Zeichnungen*, February 5-April 8

Paris, Galerie de France, *Julio Gonzalez*, September 26-November 2.
12 sculptures, 30 drawings

Basel, *Art 9'78: Julio Gonzalez*, June 14-19. Organized by Galerie de France. Brochure.
33 sculptures, 16 drawings

Museo de Bellas Artes de Valencia, *Julio González*, May. Catalogue with text by Eusebio Sempere, reprinted text by González. Organized by Ministerio de Cultura, Madrid.
36 drawings
Traveled to Alcoy, Caja de Ahorro de Alicante y Murcia, June 27-July 8; Museo de Bellas Artes de Zaragoza, September; Tarrasa, Museo Provincial Textil, October 18-December 30; Museo de Arte Moderno de Bilbao, January 1979; Oviedo, Caja de Ahorros de Asturias, February 5-March 27; Seville, Museo de Arte Contemporáneo, November

1980

Madrid, Fundacion Juan March, *Julio González: Esculpturas y dibujos*, January-March. Catalogue with text by Germain Viatte.
66 sculptures, 45 drawings
Traveled to Barcelona, Capella de l'Antic Hospital de la Santa Creu, *Julio González: Escultures i dibuxos*, April 11-May 31. Checklist with text by Alexandre Cirici

Barcelona, Galeria Trece, *Julio González/ Joan González/ Roberta González*, December 16, 1980-January 1981. Catalogue with text by Antonio Urrutia; text by Vicente Aguilera Cerni excerpted from *Julio, Joan, Roberta González*, Barcelona, 1973.
24 paintings by Julio González

1981

Athens, Georgia Museum of Art, University of Geor-

gia, *Julio Gonzalez: Drawings and Sculptures*, February 15-March 15.
3 sculptures, 53 drawings

Mexico City, Galeria Ponce, *Julio González dibujos*, July 21-August 22. Brochure with text by Marivés Villalobos.
1 sculpture, 23 drawings

New York, The Pace Gallery, *Julio Gonzalez: Sculptures and Drawings*, October 2-31. Catalogue with text by Rosalind Krauss.
28 sculptures, 21 drawings

Museo de Monterrey, *Julio González: dibujos y esculturas*. December 15, 1981-February 15, 1982. Catalogue with text by Manuel Felguérez.
18 sculptures, 23 drawings

1982
Musée des Beaux-Arts et d'Archéologie de Rennes, *Gonzalez: Dessins et sculptures des années 30*, September 10-November 14. Organized in collaboration with Musée National d'Art Moderne, Centre Georges Pompidou, Paris. Brochure with text by Nicole Barbier.
11 sculptures, 58 drawings
Traveled to La Maison de la Culture de Chalons-sur-Saône, France, December 4-31

Basel, Galerie Beyeler, *González: Sculptures, dessins*, October-December. Catalogue with text by Jörn Merkert.
36 sculptures, 35 drawings

Madrid, Museo Español de Arte Contemporáneo, *Dibujos de Julio González*, November 16, 1982-January 17, 1983. Catalogue with texts by Susana Cangas, Alvaro Martinez-Novillo, Maria Jose Salazar, Cecilia Vidal.
194 drawings
Traveled to Barcelona, Palau de la Virreina, January 13-February 27, 1983

Vicente Aguilera Cerni, *Julio Gonzalez*, Madrid, 1971

Vicente Aguilera Cerni, *Julio, Joan, Roberta González: Itinerario de una Dinastía*, Barcelona, 1973

Léon Degand, *Gonzalez*, New York, 1959

Pierre Descargues, *Julio Gonzalez*, Paris, 1971

Jörn Merkert, *Julio Gonzalez: Werkkatalog der Skulpturen*, Berlin, forthcoming

Ricardo Perez Alfonso, *Julio González: Escultor hierro y espacio forjados*, Madrid, 1934

Josephine Withers, *Julio Gonzalez: Sculpture in Iron*, New York, 1978

EXHIBITION 83/1
5,000 copies of this catalogue, designed by Malcolm Grear Designers, typeset by Dumar Typesetting, Inc., have been printed by Eastern Press in February 1983 for the Trustees of The Solomon R. Guggenheim Foundation on the occasion of the exhibition *Julio González: A Retrospective*.

Left to right, Mme Mercereau, Alexandre Mercereau, unidentified friend, Lola, Pilar, González, unidentified friend at Mercereau's house, Gandelu, ca. 1929

PHOTOGRAPHIC CREDITS

WORKS IN THE EXHIBITION

Color

Phillipe Besacier: cat. no. 104

Courtesy Galerie Beyeler, Basel: cat. nos. 170, 226

Carmelo Guadagno and David Heald: cat. no. 204

Jacques L'Hoir: cat. nos. 40, 84, 247

Jacqueline Hyde; courtesy Musée National d'Art Moderne, Centre Georges Pompidou, Paris: cat. no. 120, cover

Francis Kompalitch; courtesy Galerie de France, Paris: cat. no. 136

Courtesy Kunsthalle der Stadt Bielefeld: cat. no. 138

Courtesy Fondation Maeght, Saint-Paul-de-Vence: cat. no. 154

Courtesy Museo Español de Arte Contemporáneo, Madrid: cat. no. 126

Courtesy Musée National d'Art Moderne, Centre Georges Pompidou, Paris: cat. no. 68

Lee Statsworth; courtesy Hirshhorn Museum and Sculpture Garden, Smithsonian Institution, Washington, D.C.: cat. no. 92

Courtesy Stedelijk Museum, Amsterdam: cat. no. 201

Black and White

Courtesy The Art Institute of Chicago, Illinois: cat. no. 106

Courtesy The Baltimore Museum of Art: cat. no. 88

Courtesy Dr. W. A. Bechtler, Zollikon: cat. nos. 159, 186

Courtesy Galerie Beyeler, Basel: cat. nos. 97, 173, 181

Klaus Burkhard: cat. no. 135

Geoffrey Clements: cat. no. 121

Prudence Cuming Ass. Ltd.: cat. nos. 76, 131, 184

Courtesy Fogg Art Museum, Harvard University, Cambridge, Massachusetts: cat. no. 175

Courtesy Galerie de France, Paris: cat. no. 57, 71, 78, 82, 177, 191, 206, 208, 227, 251, 252

Claude Gaspari: cat. nos. 183, 189, 213, 244, 245

Studio Photo Gérald, Vézelay: cat. no. 137

Julio González: cat. no. 58

Carmelo Guadagno: cat. nos. 105a, b, 218, 253

François Guilbaud: cat. nos. 1, 39, 59, 67, 81a, 90a, 111, 116, 131, 151, 157, 160, 161, 195, 196b, 209, 225, 228, 238

Courtesy Paul Haim, Paris: cat. nos. 190a, b

Courtesy Hans Hartung, Antibes: cat. nos. 86, 102, 134, 179, 207, 210, 215 a-d, 219, 220, 230, 231, 246

David Heald: cat. no. 23

Jacques L'Hoir: cat. nos. 11a, b, 14a, b, 15, 22, 28, 29, 31, 33, 57, 81b, 176, 211

Jacqueline Hyde: cat. nos. 155, 165, 168, 221

Bernd Kirtz, BFF: cat. no. 103

Courtesy Kunsthaus Zürich, cat. no. 112

Courtesy The Arthur and Madeleine Lejwa Collection, New York: cat. no. 108

Courtesy Madeleine Lejwa, New York: cat. no. 100

Courtesy Fondation Maeght, Saint-Paul-de-Vence: cat. no. 236

Courtesy Galerie Carmen Martinez, Paris: cat. no. 122

Robert E. Mates: cat. no. 87

Micko: cat. no. 123

Courtesy Moderna Museet, Stockholm: cat. nos. 47, 146-149

Al Mozell; courtesy The Pace Gallery, New York: cat. nos. 169a, b

Courtesy Musée National d'Art Moderne, Centre Georges Pompidou, Paris: cat. nos. 6, 20, 21, 25, 51, 89, 130, 150, 156, 162, 174, 222

Courtesy Museo de Arte Moderno, Barcelona: cat. nos. 2, 9, 10, 12, 16, 17-19, 24, 34, 37, 42, 47, 48, 52, 53, 60, 64, 65, 73, 74, 79, 94, 95, 101, 187, 216, 232, 248

Courtesy Museo Español de Arte Contemporáneo, Madrid: cat. nos. 7, 26, 27, 30, 35, 49, 50, 54, 55, 75, 80, 145, 153, 180, 229, 249

Courtesy The Museum of Fine Arts, Houston: cat. no. 233

Courtesy The Museum of Modern Art, New York: cat. nos. 163, 164, 166, 188, 192, 193

Otto E. Nelson: cat. nos. 32, 152, 182, 185

Pierre van Oudhenove, Monthyon: cat. nos. 5, 8

Courtesy The Pace Gallery, New York: cat. nos. 217, 235

Courtesy Philadelphia Museum of Art: cat. no. 125

Courtesy Rijksmuseum Kröller-Müller, Otterlo: cat. no. 214

Schroeter, Hammer and Trog: cat. no. 129

Courtesy The Trustees of the Tate Gallery, London: cat. nos. 60, 132, 143, 158, 178

Jerry Thompson: cat. no. 237

F. Valentini: cat. nos. 77a, 96a

François Walch: cat. nos. 3, 36a-d, 38, 41, 43-45, 66a, c, 69, 72a, b, 76b, 83a, b, 85, 90b, 96b, 98, 99, 107a-g, 110, 113, 118a-c, 119, 144, 167, 171, 172, 196a, 197-200, 202, 203, 205, 211, 212, 234, 239-243b, 250, 254

Courtesy Winston-Malbin Collection, New York: cat. nos. 91, 109

FIGURES IN THE TEXT

Courtesy Dr. W. A. Bechtler, Zollikon: p. 186

Jean Bescos; courtesy Pierrette Gargallo Anguera: figs. 1, 2

Jean Bescos; courtesy Musée National d'Art Moderne, Centre Georges Pompidou, Paris: fig. 3

J. E. Bulloz: p. 195

Jean Dubout; courtesy Susi Magnelli, Meudon: figs. 14, 15

Documentation photographique de la Réunion des Musées nationaux, Paris: figs. 4, 5, 7, 9-13

Courtesy González Estate Archive, Paris: p. 162

Jacqueline Hyde; courtesy Musée National d'Art Moderne, Centre Georges Pompidou, Paris: p. 189

Courtesy Rosalind Krauss: p. 82

Courtesy Alex Maguy, Paris: fig. 11

Henri Mardyks; courtesy Maya Widmaier, Marseilles: fig. 8

Courtesy Carmen Martinez and Viviane Grimminger, Paris: pp. 8, 11, 12, 15, 211, 213

Courtesy The Trustees of the Tate Gallery, London: fig. 6

Marc Vaux: p. 216

François Walch: p. 87

All works by González and Magnelli © A.D.A.G.P., Paris, 1983

All works by Gargallo and Picasso © S.P.A.D.E.M., Paris/V.A.G.A., New York, 1983